ONE
HUMAN
RACE

ONE HUMAN RACE

FIVE STAGES TO EMPOWERING
TRANSFORMATIVE CHANGE

Jeff McGee, Ed.D.

BMcTALKS Press
4980 South Alma School Road
Suite 2-493
Chandler, Arizona 85248

Copyright © 2020 by Jeff McGee, Ed.D. All rights reserved.

No part of this publication may be reproduced, stored in a retrieval system, or transmitted in any form or by any means, electronic, mechanical, photocopying, recording, scanning, or otherwise without the prior written permission of the Publisher. Requests to the Publisher for permissions should be submitted to the Permissions Department, BMcTALKS Press, 4980 S. Alma School Road, Ste 2-493, Chandler, AZ 85248 or at www.bmctalkspress.com/permissions

The views expressed in this publication are those of the author; are the responsibility of the author; and do not necessarily reflect or represent the views of BMcTALKS Press, its owner, or its independent contractors.

Volume pricing is available to bulk orders placed by corporations, associations, and others. For details, please contact BMcTALKS Press at info@bmtpress.com

ESV, The Holy Bible, English Standard Version is adapted from the Revised Standard Version of the Bible, copyright Division of Christian Education of the National Council of the Churches of Christ in the U.S.A. All rights reserved.

KJV, King James Version. Public domain.

NASB, New American Standard Bible Copyright © 1960, 1962, 1963, 1968, 1971, 1972, 1973, 1975, 1977, 1995 by The Lockman Foundation, La Habra, Calif. All rights reserved.

NIV, Holy Bible, New International Version®, NIV® Copyright © 1973, 1978, 1984, 2011 by Biblica, Inc.® Used by permission. All rights reserved worldwide.

NLT, Holy Bible, New Living Translation, copyright © 1996, 2004, 2015 by Tyndale House Foundation. Used by permission of Tyndale House Publishers, Inc., Carol Stream, Illinois 60188. All rights reserved.

Small references from my dissertation were used in this book. See McGee, D. J. (2018). *Cross-Cultural Dynamics Among White-led Nonprofit Organizations in South Phoenix Communities of Color.* Doctoral dissertation. Northern Arizona University.

FIRST EDITION

Library of Congress Control Number: 2020918242

Paperback: 978-1-953315-04-5
eBook: 978-1-953315-05-2

Cover and interior design by Medlar Publishing Solutions Pvt Ltd., India.

Printed in the United States of America.

DEDICATION

To my parents who supported me down through the years in my goal of achieving my purpose.

To my son who motivates me to keep working hard and doing more.

To every person who has fought and/or died in their quests for all humanity to be treated equally and fairly.

To you, the reader, for whom I desire to come to fully know and realize Christ's love for you and all humanity regardless of age, race, color, religion, sex, sexual orientation, national orientation, and ability.

To all who have experienced and fell victim to the sin of racism and oppression.

To all humanity being united as one race and loving our neighbors as Christ has commanded.

ONE HUMAN RACE

FIVE STAGES TO EMPOWERING TRANSFORMATIVE CHANGE

The 2020 protests sparked by the murder of George Floyd and others in police custody have brought the issue of racism in the United States front and center. You'd think that of all groups in the United States that Christian churches, even those that are predominantly white, with their message of Jesus Christ's love for his flock, would be free of racism. As a black man who works with pastors, Christian leaders, and their staff in all sectors, I can attest that this is simply not the case, despite the biblical injunction to do so.

In the New Testament, Jesus proclaims that loving your neighbor is the second greatest commandment. If this commandment is so important—and almost every Christian knows this—then why is it so hard for us to obey? The church as a whole has struggled, whether consciously or unconsciously, throughout the years with this thing called race and ethnicity.

From a kingdom-of-God perspective, as Christians, we *should* do better. We *must* do better. We aren't going to do better, however, if we don't change our ways. Based on my experiences working in Christian nonprofits, conducting hundreds of hours of consulting and trainings, and my academic studies, I've developed practical methods to promote biblically based cross-cultural work and to overcome racism. But first, we need to understand how we got here.

My fellow brothers and sisters in Christ, there is no division in the kingdom of God when it comes to race, but somehow the church has managed to continually use it to promote division. In 1 Corinthians 1:10 (NIV), it reads, "I appeal to you, brothers and sisters, in the name of our Lord Jesus Christ, that all of you agree with one another in what you say and that there be *no divisions among you*, but that you be perfectly united in mind and thought" (emphasis added). The question I want to propose is this.

Does the world hate the church because it stands against the sin of racism, or has the church joined the world in its ideologies of racism here in the United States?

TABLE OF CONTENTS

Preface xi

PART ONE
How Did We Get Here?
The History of Christian Racism in the United States

CHAPTER 1
Race and Ethnicity: A Biblical Perspective 3

CHAPTER 2
Race and the Concept of Race. 9

CHAPTER 3
From Race to Racism 25

PART TWO
How Systemic Racism Works in Practice

CHAPTER 4
My Story: A Personal Perspective 47

PART THREE
How the Christian Church Can Address Racism and Learn to Work Across Cultures

CHAPTER 5
The Challenge of Cross-Cultural Interactions 59

CHAPTER 6
Building Cross-Cultural Collaboration 69

References. *137*

PREFACE

In August 2009, my understanding of the church changed forever. I had recently rededicated my life back to Jesus Christ after walking away from the faith for many years. My experience, while shocking, led me to find my purpose in life and led me on a journey that I have passionately pursued ever since.

I had never been to Fresno, California, and was excited to visit some friends there. I was simply passing through, so my stay was brief. I happened to arrive in the city about the time their church was moving the service from a building to an outdoor park in a local neighborhood. As it was explained to me, the neighborhood was an under-resourced and underserved community. I had never been to something like this before, but because I was in town, I gladly went to volunteer at the church service that warm, summer morning. I loved the idea of taking the gospel to the people, as opposed to waiting for the people to come to the church. Not only was the church taking the gospel message to the people, it also was serving free meals, renting bouncy houses, and providing many other activities for the kids, including a small petting zoo.

I had arrived with my friends with the goal of helping serve from the beginning to the end of the event. There were many people from the neighborhood who came out that day. They arrived in waves, it seemed. People sat at tables, on lawn chairs, and on the grass, and some leaned against large, shady trees. It was a beautiful scene to see the choir leading the people in worship, the pastor sharing the gospel message, and the people responding by dedicating their lives to Jesus Christ. Afterwards, everyone shared a meal together while the kids enjoyed the great activities. It was during this time that I met Albert, a Mexican-American man. He was a member of the multicultural church and was grateful that his church was doing this service in the neighborhood. He said to me that he wouldn't have missed this event for anything in the world. As we talked, he then shared his story with me that forever changed my life.

He began by saying that he hadn't been a Christian all his life. He used to live in the streets and was homeless for many years. He lost his job, wife, and children due to his addiction to crack cocaine. "I was an addict," he said with a serious look on his face. "I got caught up with drugs and didn't see it coming." He went on to say that it wasn't until he hit rock bottom and almost took his own life that he sought help. I was not prepared for what he said next. He stated, "I went to several churches to seek help and was turned away!" My jaw dropped!

I asked him to repeat what he said in hopes that I heard him wrong. He repeated what he originally said. I asked him to please elaborate on what happened. He gladly shared with me that he went to several churches and was told, "You have to become a member for us to help you," and "You are not dressed appropriately to attend the service," and "You have to wear a suit and tie," and "You need to be off drugs before we can help you," and the one that really affected me "You need to find a church with people of your own race."

I stood there in complete and utter shock! At first, part of me didn't believe him, but there was something about him. His gentle smile and sincere demeanor were calming and peaceful. His polite manners and humble spirit showed he was present to volunteer and serve others. I could tell that God was with him. I didn't know what to say. I was speechless. My heart was heavy. My heart was hurting. Before I knew it, tears began to flow down my face. I never thought in a million years that churches in America would reject people from hearing the gospel; reject those seeking help, those who wanted to worship, and those who wanted to live in community with other believers.

Albert went on to say that it wasn't until he found his current church that he received the help he needed, which led to being drug free and a believer in Jesus Christ. Because of the support his church gave him, he volunteers as much time as he can within the outreach ministry and enjoys sharing his story with everyone in hopes they find Jesus also.

On my flight back to the East Coast, I could not get his story out of my head. Tears would flow down my face every time I thought of him, but more tragically, when I thought of the state of the church and what it means to be a follower of Christ. Even when I shared his story with my friends and family months and years later, I found myself getting emotional about the thought of what he went through. I became angry at the church.

Is this an accurate depiction of what the church has become in America? Is it like this abroad? Is it more a gathering of followers of Christ in a social club than a place of worship, teaching, and building true community? Have church parishioners become so privileged that they dictate who can come in and who cannot? Questions regarding what it means to be a follower of Christ started circulating through my mind. I questioned the church and, quite honestly, I still question the church. This experience began my journey to find truth and discover the barriers that we need to overcome as the body of Christ.

Since my experience in 2009, I have conducted many years of research, including historical, content analysis, theoretical, and empirical, to better understand the past that has directly influenced and affected our present. Within the context of the United States (including the church), the concept of race is by far the biggest historical and present-day contributor to division compared with any other category that causes division. Because of this fact, I will discuss race as an example of culture, but I will reference the term *culture* throughout. I conceptualize the term culture as a broader concept that includes race and other diverse categories, such as ethnicity, gender, nationality, age, and others.

The goal of this book is twofold: first, to provide readers with a deeper understanding of culture, using race as a model, to illustrate how human theories and practices have caused division within the body of Christ; and second, to introduce a framework for developing biblically based cross-cultural unity and collaboration. Based on the data collected through personal experiences, research, stories from church parishioners and non-church people, church and nonprofit leadership teams, board members, and deacons, I have developed a model to support the body of Christ as we navigate through cultural differences with the goal of unity.

By implementing this model, leaders are given the skills and tools needed to understand themselves and others, and to create cross-cultural communities through unity. To do so, you must understand yourself, understand others, and understand cross-cultural unity and collaboration. In this book, I will use examples from the education and nonprofit sectors to help illustrate theories, concepts, and ideas. It is important to realize that using examples from different sectors can help deepen understanding and further illustrate points.

You can come to knowing yourself only with deep reflection. For some of us, that's easy, but for the majority of us, it's difficult, dreadful, and sometimes painful. Author B. J. Neblett (2009) once said, "We are the sum total of our experiences. Those experiences—be they positive or negative—make us the person we are, at any given point in our lives." Rick Warren (2002) said, "We are products of our past, but we don't have to be prisoners of it." How we behave is a clear indication of what we have experienced and what we have learned. Therefore, what we have learned and experienced are the driving forces behind not only how we behave, but how we perpetuate those behaviors on our children, family, friends, and community. This includes what we have learned about race and culture and also how that has influenced our biases, stereotypes, prejudices, worldview, privileges, and more to give us a solid foundation of how we think, act, and react.

Understanding others takes work. It's intentional. It's purposeful. It's deliberate. It's methodical. In our individualistic society and culture, it is the antithesis of what we do, who we are, what we see, and how our reality operates. When we accept Christ in our lives, it is an individual decision that we make, but to live out our faith is done in a collective community. Hebrews 10:24–25 (NIV) tells us "And let us consider how we may spur one another on toward love and good deeds, not giving up meeting together, as some are in the habit of doing, but encouraging one another—and all the more as you see the Day approaching."

To build healthy relationships and collaborations across races as followers of Christ, we have to move outside our comfort zones and build relationships with those of a different racial makeup than what we are used to. The Bible, from Genesis to Revelation, illustrates

God's direct intention for all people to reconcile to him regardless of racial differences and do it within the context of cross-cultural community. Once we begin to understand others, we are more open to accepting them and fulfilling the commandment to love our neighbor.

Building relationships across races is a lot easier when we first understand ourselves *before* we begin to understand others. Applying racial unity and collaboration to serve and uplift/empower/transform individuals and communities through relationships details how we unite as one in the kingdom of God to further the gospel message. It's through this process that we develop a true, authentic appreciation and understanding of how we are to love one another.

We develop competencies on how to build systems of racial well-being and leverage the diverse gifts within the body of Christ across cultures. We are equipped to break down systems of oppression and marginalization that hold back our brothers and sisters in Christ from justice and true equality. Eric Mason, in his book *Woke Church*, wrote, "Scripture makes it clear that we are supposed to be totally awake to what is happening in our world and steadfast in our commitment to fulfill the great commandments."

Chapter 1 explores a biblical perspective on race and identify a framework for God's meaning behind race. For leaders to understand how to dismantle systemic racism, we must understand race.

Chapter 2 gives insight into the often-confused idea of race and the concept of race in the United States. By developing competencies around the concept of race, we can then understand how racism is embedded deep in the foundation of the United States.

Chapter 3 identifies terms and phrases that are often misunderstood and lead to frustration, anger, and avoidance. Leaders who grasp these terms can more effectively embark on recreating organizational systems, policies, and processes that are inclusive.

Chapter 4 introduces you to my personal perspectives and my journey over the past decade. I wanted to include a personal touch so you can begin to understand my experiences.

Chapter 5 discusses cross-cultural interactions, specifically a conceptual definition of culture, white supremacy, and deficit thinking. Again, by understanding these ideologies, we can better communicate across cultures and reduce barriers to collaboration and relationship-building efforts.

Chapter 6 describes the cross-cultural model of collaboration. This model serves leaders who are dismantling or seeking to dismantle systemic racism within their individual lives, churches, and communities. The five stages of the model introduce clear steps that leaders can use to teach and empower their teams for transformative change.

PART ONE

HOW DID WE GET HERE? THE HISTORY OF CHRISTIAN RACISM IN THE UNITED STATES

To understand how we can overcome racism in the Christian church, we need to understand what we mean by *race* and *racism*; how racism was present from the beginning in the United States; the contributions of early Christian Europeans in establishing the concept of race; and what we can learn from the Bible about unity, collaboration, and love.

CHAPTER 1

RACE AND ETHNICITY: A BIBLICAL PERSPECTIVE

If we are to overcome racism in the Christian church, we must first understand the complex, confusing, and sometimes contradictory ways that race and ethnicity are understood. Dein (2006) refers to race as "the social group a person belongs to on account of a mix of physical characteristics" and refers to ethnicity as "the social group a person belongs to based on a shared culture" (p. 68). Ethnicity is more fluid. According to experts, the consensus is that we do have control over our ethnicity. For example, we understand that it is mostly our choice what religion we practice or where we want to live or what language(s) we speak. Another example is the choice to identify physical characteristics such as bloodline. For example, if a person is Kenyan and Mexican, that person could choose either identify from which to self-identify. The key takeaway for ethnicity is the association with how someone identifies learned traits of him- or herself.

Race, on the other hand, is based on less changeable characteristics. The skin color associated with race is applied to people based solely on the way they look. It's merely associated with one's skin color and sometimes other physical traits. The color of one's skin is solely attributed to the amount of melanin, which is the pigment that gives human skin, eyes, and hair their color. Dark-skinned people have more melanin in their skin than light-skinned people. The amount of melanin in skin makes it the color it is.

Simply put, what has caused major divisions between people for thousands of years boils down to the fact that some people have more melanin in their skin than others. Think about that for a moment. Hate is spewed between races over something as simple as the amount of melanin in someone's skin. Why should the amount of melanin in one's skin incite such hatred, discrimination, injustice, and animosity? Further, from a biblical worldview, why are there different races in the world if we are all descendants of Adam? And how are we to understand and embrace race to further contribute to the kingdom of God?

WHY SO MANY RACES?

To answer this question, we must go back to the beginning, when God created Adam. This is probably one of the first Bible lessons we learned in Sunday school. We understand that God created Adam from dust and breathed life into him, and he became a living human being (Genesis 2:7). To provide insight into race, we need to flip to Acts 17:26 (NIV), which reads, "From one man [Adam] he [God] made every nation of men, that they should inhabit the whole earth; and he determined the times set for them and the exact places where they should live." From this scripture, we get three critical points:

1. God made **one** man. 2. Through that one man, **every** nation was created, and they should inhabit the whole earth. 3. God determined **when** and **where** they should live. (The word *man* does not signify being male but is representative of humankind.) The Bible makes it clear that there is only one race, the human race.

One of the most common fallacies is that some people evolved at different times, locations, and even from different species. The Bible clearly debunks that theory. God created one man, and through him, all men were created. In the King James Version, the beginning of Acts 17:26 says it like this: "and hath made of one blood all nations of men." Adam is the one man whereby all humankind derives. God made one man from the dust and never did that again. Even Jesus, in all his glory and splendor as God, had to abide by the law of human nature, which was to be born of a woman through birth. Again, the Bible makes it clear that there is only one race, the human race.

THROUGH THAT ONE MAN, EVERY NATION WAS CREATED AND THEY SHOULD INHABIT THE WHOLE EARTH

It is important to understand that God is the founder of nations, not man. Man inhabits nations, manages nations, rules nations, and so forth, but the purpose by which God established nations was for man to dwell and manage the land (Genesis 1:26). Therefore, the purpose for man is to work or cultivate the land (nations) in relationship with the founder, God, for the preservation and the mutual benefit of humankind.

Science confirms that man originated in Africa, although exactly where is still debated. Although nations were created over the whole earth, the human race is still connected through that one man, Adam.

In essence, we are all connected through the blood of Adam, the original father of the human race. So, whether man lives in China, South Africa, Netherlands, Canada, Chile, and so forth, we are all connected because we originated from the same place and the same person. One race!

What does this mean for our understanding of nation and immigration? Without addressing my own personal views and in reference to the above scripture, we have to ask ourselves: Whose nation is it really? From a biblical perspective, then, if God is the founder and humans are the managers of nations, whose practices and policies should be used to determine who, when, and how a human being can enter another nation? Because God is the founder, he is the owner, not human beings, therefore we need to ask, "What does God say about immigration?" (To get you started, look at Deuteronomy 10:19, Roman 12:13, Matthew 25:35, Zechariah 7:9–10, and Ezekiel 47:22.) Many people have left the church altogether because a church stood either for or against immigration. I am not making a debate here, but if we are to understand how to work across cultures, we have to begin challenging, from a biblical perspective, our beliefs and norms that are underlying our behaviors.

GOD DETERMINED WHEN AND WHERE THEY SHOULD LIVE

To understand when and where man should live, we need to recount the stories of the great flood and the Tower of Babel. After God sent the flood to destroy man, he reserved the family of Noah to rebuild or repopulate the earth. After the flood ended, there were only eight people left on earth: Noah, Noah's wife, his three sons, and their wives. In Genesis 9:18–19 (NIV) it reads, "The sons of Noah who came out of the ark were Shem, Ham and Japheth. (Ham was the father of Canaan.) These were the three sons of Noah, and from them came the people who were scattered over the earth."

The story of the Tower of Babel involves scattering as well. In Genesis 11:7–8 (NIV) we read, "Come let us go down and confuse their language so they will not understand each other. So, the Lord scattered them from there over all the earth and they stopped building the city." In these two passages, we see that God dispersed man all over the earth with the intention that man should not live in one place (meaning one nation).

That doesn't mean that the human race is now divided. We are still one race but now dwelling in different locations throughout the earth. The same biblical mandates that applied to the human race at Babel still remain for the human race that scattered throughout the earth. Remembering that God is the founder of all nations, one nation is not better than other nations, especially within the context of race.

HOW DID SKIN COLORS BECOME WHAT THEY ARE?

That people are scattered explains why skin color is different around the world. Skin color variations are influenced by certain elements such as climate, environment, diet, and sun exposure. For example, longer exposure to ultraviolet rays, such as those near the equator, can be damaging to the skin, but the higher melanin content of darker skin provides greater protection against skin penetration by ultraviolet rays than the lower melanin content of lighter skin. People with darker skin live closer to the equator, and as you get farther and farther from the equator, people have lighter skin. Still one race, the human race.

CHAPTER 2

RACE AND THE CONCEPT OF RACE

Most people, including me, have misunderstood the term *race*. As it was stated previously, race is a term applied to people based solely on the way they look. I am considered a light-skinned black man. To that, I have struggled throughout my life with being identified by others as too light to be "black" and too dark to be "white." I was theoretically caught along the fence, and it has been difficult for me to find a racial space where I can say I fully belong. In full transparency, I still struggle with this even now because of humans' innate desire to classify people into categories so they can establish meaning.

This is what is referred to as the concept of race, which at its most basic meaning, establishes criteria to make meaning of specific skin colors of people. Think about your time in science class in elementary school. One of the first lessons was to understand how to classify things such as mammals, birds, amphibians, and so forth. As human beings, we have a natural tendency to classify things so we can make meaning of them. For example, if we are walking down the street and see a turtle on the sidewalk, our brain classifies it as an animal that is relatively harmless and adorable in some ways, so we react to it accordingly. If we are walking down the street and see a lion standing on the sidewalk, our brain classifies it as an animal that is dangerous, so we react to it accordingly. So goes the same philosophy with race.

Since the "discovery" of the New World, the idea of classifying people by their skin color was simply used as a descriptor or identifier. Table 1 (Michigan State University, The Rise of Scientific Racial Ideology [1492–1890]) gives us a great timeline of how the formation of race or the understanding of different skin colors was developed from the late 1490s until the late 1890s. Although this table doesn't encompass all historical decisions and the impact that societal, economic, and political factors have on race, it helps build some understanding of the development of race.

Because human beings have to make meaning of things, race, then, had to be labeled as something that has meaning; therefore, human beings created the concept of race. The concept of race is solely a human creation! Ta-Nehisi Coates stated, "Race is the child of racism, not the father." What he is referring to here is the concept of race. As humankind has done for centuries, in sin, we take what God meant for good and perverted it for evil.

Referencing our discussion on the Tower of Babel, all humankind is labeled as the human race. When the people were dispersed throughout the entire world, they still were the human race. That did not change! Humankind throughout time, however, has conducted countless years of research and developed numerous theories to try to prove one part of the human race is less than the other. A breakdown of the human race into racial categories is simply a human way of "making up people."

Table 1 *The Rise of Scientific Racial Ideology (1492–1890)*

1492	Discovery of New World prompts questions about the nature of people and customs of Native Americans	Although the Irish had been called a "race" previously, the word had not been applied to different peoples anywhere before this.
1493	Peter Martyr, an Italian working for Ferdinand and Isabella of Spain, compiles all the reports of new peoples he can gather.	Published in early 1500s, his works were available to other scholars and to the Roman Catholic Church. He created a short vocabulary list of Taino Indian (Puerto Ricans are descendants of Taino Indians) words.
late 1500s	First taxonomic systems for human populations	Giordano Bruno and Jean Bodin sort people based on skin color. The descriptions were purely descriptive of color and were ideologically neutral.
1550s	Further taxonomies develop	Bernard Varen and John Ray sort humans into categories according to stature, shape, food habits, and skin color. The vocabulary used is neutral: e.g, types, varieties, peolpes, nations, species
1641	Non-human primates are "discovered"	First published account of a chimpanzee
1658	Non-human primates are "discovered"	First published account of an orangutan
1684	First (perhaps) taxonomy for humans emphasized physical traits	François Bernier published an article in a French journal. Four types were identified: Europeans, Far Easterners, Negroes, and Lapps. He was creating these categories purely from "stories" recorded by travelers. He did not use the word "race."
late 1600s	The word "race" appears in various writings in reference to "breed" and "generations"	

(continued)

Table 1 *The Rise of Scientific Racial Ideology (1492–1890) (continued)*

1690	A "pygmy" arrives in England	Edward Tyson demonstrates the similarity between humans and primates
1700	Educated people searched backwards through literature for "evidence" of racial thinking	
1735	Swedish botanist Carolus Linnaeus publishes *Systemae Naturna*. This work classifies all living things into a vast system of categories. This system is still in use today. It is the basis for all scientific naming of species.	Linnaeus creates four varieties of the genus "homo"—Europeaus, Americanus, Asiaticus and Africanus (plus a few miscellaneous categories for unexplained beings like "wild men" and "dwarfs"). He describes these varieties with some very charged terms like "avaricious" for Asiaticus. He does not use the word "race." Like Bernier, Linnaeus was creating his system from the records passed on to him. His actual experience was limited to Europeans.
1749	Comte de Buffon introduces the term "race" into the natural sciences.	He invents these categories: Laplanders, Tartars or Mongolians, southern Asiatics, Europeans, Ethiopians, Malays. He saw humans as a single species and theorized that climate was the "chief cause of the different colours of men."
1770–1781	Joann Blumenbach, a professor of medicine in Germany proposes fours varieties of man: Caucasian, Mongolian, Ethiopian, American and Malay.	He believed all peoples derived from a single origin, an Adam and Eve, if you will. This is called monogenesis. Degeneration caused the differences. Blumenbach did not believe the varieties could be neatly divided.
Late 18th century	Philosophers and politicians build a theory of race; scientists participate wholeheartedly.	Thinkers from Thomas Jefferson to Benjamin Rush (a founding father) to Immanuel Kant postulate on the inferiority of non-European races.
1776	American Revolution	Codifies African Americans as inferior.

1789	French Revolution	Propels all of Europe into war. 13 year revolution—mainly France, Spain and Britain.
1791	Haitian Revolution	Saint Domingue, Haiti, starts revolution when French planters would not grant their slaves citizenship as decreed by the National Assembly of France in "Declaration of the Rights of Man."
1799	Charles White, an English physician, publishes *An Account of the Regular Gradation in Man*	Uses the Great Chain of Being as an explanation for race. He believes in *polygenisis*, that is that the various races originated separately. There was no Adam and Eve.
1800	Gabriel Prosser's Conspiracy	Causes more apprehension in the South about the current status of Africans.
1817	Baron George Cuvier, a French zoologist, corresponds with Thomas Jefferson.	Concludes ancient Egyptians could not have been African.
1822	Denmark Vesey's Rebellion	George Wilson, "a favourite and confidential slave," informs master of planned insurrection of thousands of free and enslaved Africans who lived in and around Charleston, SC.
1839	Samuel Morton, a Philadelphia physician and anatomist, publishes *Crania Americanan* and *Crania Agyptiaca* (1844). He believes the "hybridity" of humans (the ability of different races to reproduce contradicts the laws of nature. Morton is considered a hero in the southern states.	A polygenist, Morton influenced an entire generation of American race scientists: Josiah Nott, Louis Agassiz, a Harvard scientist, George R. Gliddon, William Pickering, Charles Caldwell, J. Aitken Meigs, Samuel Cartwright, Frederick L. Hoffman. In Europe, the field was filled with men like: Lord Kames, Charles Hamilton Smith, Robert Knox, Paul Broca (founder of the Anthropoligical Society of Paris).

(continued)

Table 1 *The Rise of Scientific Racial Ideology (1492–1890) (continued)*

1820s	Phrenology is all the fad.	Scientists and parlor entertainers believe you can determine a person's character from the shape of his/her skull. Franz Joseph Gall and Jacob Spurzheim invented this pseudo-science. It is easy to see how the sciences of "somatometry" (describing differences based on bodily dimensions) and "anthropometry" (differences based on skull dimensions) developed after this.
1800s	Monogenists fostered racial classifications but were more liberal in their beliefs.	Samuel Stanhope Smith, Reverend John Bachman, James Cowles Prichard, Sir William Laurence, and others felt the polygenist position contradicted Christian belief.
1807	England and the United States outlaw the slave trade on the high seas.	
1813–83	German composer Richard Wagner proselytizes anti-Semitism and racism.	
1850s	Illegal slave trade to U.S. flourishes.	
1850s	Herbert Spencer is the self-educated editor of *The Economist*. This journal is still very influential today in conservative circles.	Spencer fosters the idea of "survival of the fittest" before Darwin publishes his classic. Darwin's work is later misinterpreted to support Spencer's ideas. For Spencer, human progress was the result of competition and struggle. He opposed labor unions, industrial regulation, public education, women's rights, charity, child labor laws, taxation, and even sanitation laws.
1855	French aristocrat Comte Joseph-Arthur de Gobineau published a famous essay, "Essay on the Inequality of Races."	Divides world's people into three races: white, yellow, and black. All civilizations were the product of the white race.

1859	Darwin's *The Origin of Species*	Darwin does not propose dividing humans into races, but pseudo-scientists insist on using his ideas to bolster the idea of race hierarchy. These people come to be known as Social Darwinists.
1869	Darwin's half-cousin, Sir Francis Galton, is one of the most famous Social Darwinists, publishes *Hereditary Genius*, claiming that certain aristocratic British families were inherently superior.	Galton coins the term "eugenics."
1880s	Alfred Binet, a French psychologist, invents "IQ."	"IQ" continues to be tied to race as in the 1990s book *The Bell Curve*.
1860s	Psychometrics fosters the notion that the brain is the seat of all intelligence and moral development	
1890	Richard Wagner's British son-in-law, Houston Stewart Chamberlain, becomes the chief disseminator of German racial superiority.	Chamberlain's *Foundations of the Nineteenth Century* became the bible of the Nazi Party.

Though racism certainly existed in the Old World, it came to a kind of perfection in the New World. It is easily argued and supported by research that the United States of America was constructed and built on a foundation of racism. Many race experts agree that racism is so engrained into the fabric of the United States that when it is protested or debated for change, many whites believe they are actually protesting against the United States. David Roediger (2019) states, "The world got along without race for the overwhelming majority of its history. The US has never been without it." Professors Omi and Winant (2014) argue that the concept of race was the fundamental organizing structure created by early European immigrants to the Western Hemisphere. To understand this, we need to dive deeper into the racial construction of the United States.

Many Europeans immigrated in the 1500s and 1600s to what is now the United States to find religious freedom, while some immigrated seeking prosperity. It is important to have an understanding of what was going on in Europe during this time. Christianity, specifically the conflict between Protestant and Catholic Europeans, was arguably the key motivating factor for the majority of Europeans escaping the region and immigrating to North America. An exhibition ("Religion and the Founding of the American Republic") from the Library of Congress stated the following.

> The religious persecution that drove settlers from Europe to the British North American colonies sprang from the conviction, held by Protestants and Catholics alike, that uniformity of religion must exist in any given society. This conviction rested on the belief that there was one true religion and that it was the duty of the civil authorities to impose it, forcibly if necessary, in the interest of saving the souls of all citizens …

The dominance of the concept, denounced by Roger Williams as "inforced uniformity of religion," meant majority religious groups who controlled political power punished dissenters in their midst. In some areas Catholics persecuted Protestants, in others Protestants persecuted Catholics, and in still others Catholics and Protestants persecuted wayward coreligionists. Although England renounced religious persecution in 1689, it persisted on the European continent. Religious persecution, as observers in every century have commented, is often bloody and implacable and is remembered and resented for generations.

There are three key points we must deduce from this if we are to better understand the formation of the concept of race in the United States. First, Christianity was the main motivating factor for Europeans fleeing Europe. It was in the name of Jesus Christ that an ongoing battle between Catholics and Protestants persisted in determining who is right and who is wrong. It was this notion that one true religion must exist in any given society to establish political, social, and economic power and to save souls.

Second, it was this whatever-it-takes mindset that included the genocide of indigenous people, if necessary, to enforce beliefs and bring Christian uniformity within a given society. An example of this is the doctrine of Manifest Destiny. The Manifest Destiny was birthed in the mid-1800s, and the belief was that the United States was "destined by God to take over other peoples and lands" (Martínez, 2016). Martínez concludes that "The arrogance of asserting that God gave white people (primarily men) the right to dominate everything around them still haunts our society and sustains its racist oppression."

Third, Christianity was noticeably divided into two sects during the course of the 1700s: Catholics and Protestants. As we later will understand, although they were separated, they both had three beliefs in common: the unity of humankind, the intriguing belief in superiority, and the understanding of exclusivity.

The reading continues from the Library of Congress.

> Many of the British North American colonies that eventually formed the United States of America were settled in the seventeenth century by men and women, who, in the face of European persecution, refused to compromise passionately held religious convictions and fled Europe. The New England colonies, New Jersey, Pennsylvania, and Maryland were conceived and established "as plantations of religion." Some settlers who arrived in these areas came for secular motives—"to catch fish" as one New Englander put it—but the great majority left Europe to worship God in the way they believed to be correct. They enthusiastically supported the efforts of their leaders to create "a city on a hill" or a "holy experiment," whose success would prove that God's plan for his churches could be successfully realized in the American wilderness. Even colonies like Virginia, which were planned as commercial ventures, were led by entrepreneurs who considered themselves "militant Protestants" and who worked diligently to promote the prosperity of the church.

Here was this idea of plantations of religion, which were areas created by leadership to build thriving societies that God would honor and that would be a simple way for others to join. We must remember here that all of this was being done in the name of Jesus Christ because of the strong desire to spread the gospel message throughout the world. We see in this passage that people were enthusiastic in supporting leaders' efforts and diligently promoting church prosperity efforts.

While these Catholic and Protestant immigrants from Europe were settling in the New World, they were faced with a perplexing issue on what to do with two specific groups of people, Africans and Indians. As Europeans came more and more in contact with Africans (through the early slave trade in Europe) and the indigenous peoples in the Americas, they were struggling between two conflicting aspirations: their need to spread the Christian gospel and their need to justify slavery, which they saw as an economic necessity.

For the Europeans in power, a system of congruity was needed as Europeans from England, France, Germany, and other countries were descending on the colonies. With all these diverse groups living in close proximity to one another in the New World, they needed to figure out a uniting way to accomplish their goals and needs. From this, the term *white* was developed as a racial classification in what is now the United States. As Rogers and Bowman (2003) state, "The term white was defined as anyone without a drop on [of] African or Indian blood. The category white was created as a political construct that was used as an organizing tool to unite Europeans in order to consolidate strength, increasing their ability to maintain control and dominance over the Native Americans and African slaves." The Virginia law of 1662 further defined that anyone with a drop of African blood was considered a slave as a hereditary, lifelong condition. The law stated this.

> WHEREAS some doubts have arrisen whether children got by any Englishman upon a negro woman should be

> slave or ffree, Be it therefore enacted and declared by this present grand assembly, that all children borne in this country shalbe held bond or free only according to the condition of the mother, And that if any christian shall committ ffornication with a negro man or woman, hee or shee so offending shall pay double the ffines imposed by the former act.

Two points to highlight from this law: First, look at how whites were described by a proper term, *Englishmen*, and the woman was described as *negro*. This gives us a glimpse into the mindset of early Europeans and how they viewed themselves and people of color. Second, look at how *Christian* was synonymous with being white and *negro* was not, thus establishing the assumption that Africans could not be Christians. Tisby (2019) stated, "Christianity became identified with the emerging concept of 'whiteness' while people of color, including indigenous people and Africans, became identified with unbelief." As Rebecca Goetz (2016) points out, "Though the Antiguan law from 1644 had pioneered the connections among lineage, religion, and race, Anglo [white]-Virginians were poised to irrevocably racialize religion, sex, and reproduction" (p. 79).

Indeed, for white Christians to justify the slavery of Africans and Indians, they debated over whether these groups of people even had souls and possessed the capacity to be Christian. Early court documents show how the categorizing of Africans and Indians as "soulless, heathen, pagan, and infidel" was influential in the determining of how they were viewed. This was common language in many court documents that showed Christian beliefs in referencing Africans and Indians. The justification that people with dark skin were subjugated to slavery didn't arise until the fifteenth century in Spain and Portugal. Haynes (2002) stated, "The application of the curse to racial slavery was the product of centuries of development in ethnic and racial stereotyping, biblical interpretation, and the history of servitude" (p. 8).

In the New World, many antebellum whites believed that Africans were incapable of self-governance and, therefore, had to be subjected to slavery and a life of servitude (Johnson, 2006). Over the course of time, as the concept of race was being further defined, whites used laws and the courts to legally justify their Christian beliefs, slavery, and their promotion of being the "better race." One such law, which was a major turning point in the classification and categorizing of Africans and Indians, was the Law of 1667 in early Virginia. The law stated, "It is enacted and declared by this grand assembly, and the authority thereof, that the conferring of baptisme doth not alter the condition of the person as to his bondage or freedome." What does this law mean?

Up until this point, baptism was synonymous with freedom and was a sign that a person was a Christian. Whether a person was African, Indian, or even a white indentured servant, upon being baptized, he or she was free both spiritually and physically. White Christians were aware of their mission to make everyone Christian (go back to the reason they left Europe). See the scripture found in Matthew 28:19 (NIV), "Therefore go and make disciples of all nations, **baptizing** them in the name of the Father and of the Son and of the Holy Spirit" (emphasis added).

According to white Christians during that time, they were still fulfilling this missionary duty, but they changed the meaning of baptism to justify slavery because of the economic benefits it brought to them. White Christians compromised the message of the gospel to justify and accommodate slavery while also, in their minds, fulfilling the mandate to make disciples (Tisby, 2019). It was a dichotomy between their Christian values and beliefs and the strong importance of maintaining power over their slaves that led them to categorize race.

As researcher Rebecca Goetz (2016) stated, "Anglo-Virginians manipulated the meaning of baptism and controlled access to baptism to redefine their own Christianity and to racialize Indians and Africans as non-Christians, a process that reverberated throughout the greater English Atlantic." This law set a precedent in motion across the colonies whereby slaves (Africans and Indians) were allowed to become Christians and be baptized but not recognized for the freedom it signified due to the economic benefits that whites received from them. Another law we can highlight is the Law of 1682, which stated the following.

> And be it further enacted by the authority aforesaid that all servants except Turkes and Moores, whilest in amity with his majesty which from and after publication of this act shall be brought or imported into this country, either by sea or land, whether Negroes, Moors, Mollattoes or Indians, who and whose parentage and native country are not christian at the time of their first purchase of such servant by some christian, although afterwards, and before such their importation and bringing into this country, they shall be converted to the christian faith; and all Indians which shall hereafter be sold by our neighbouring Indians, or any other trafiqueing with us as for slaves are hereby adjudged, deemed and taken to be slaves to all intents and purposes, any law, usage or custome to the countrary notwithstanding.

The law highlights Christianity as a foundational motivation by which all of their behaviors and beliefs followed, to the point that those who are not Christian should be converted to the Christian faith then sold into slavery. Again, emphasizing their core purposes of the Great Commission, we see the importance of them fulfilling both their desires to make everyone Christians while also justifying slavery.

CHAPTER 3

FROM RACE TO RACISM

The notion of the "white" race was created to provide unity within early European settlers who immigrated to the New World. Being white meant access to social, economic, and political opportunity, while being nonwhite meant not having access. This philosophy of race and racism became part of the fabric of the New World. The concepts of whiteness and white privilege thus led to systemic racism that was in part driven by a strong desire to dominate nonwhite groups and the expectations of assimilation.

WHITE PRIVILEGE AND WHITENESS

Recently, there has been a push by whites in power claiming that the term *white privilege* is racist and Marxist. In my experiences as a consultant and trainer, I have found that the concept of *privilege*, especially *white privilege*, has caused more division, arguments, and rifts within the body of Christ than any other term or phrase in the discussion of race and other cultural characteristics. Unfortunately, one of the main reasons why those in positions of privilege get upset is because they don't fully understand the term and context.

Let's first start with the definition of *privilege* as defined by the *Merriam-Webster* dictionary: "right or immunity granted as a peculiar benefit." Dictionary.com defines *privilege* as "a right, immunity, or benefit enjoyed only by a person beyond the advantages of most." Most people's understanding of privilege is within the context of the definitions, which is that privilege is a right. A *right*, as a noun, means something that one is morally or legally entitled to have.

For example, a husband might tell his spouse, "I worked over forty hours this week, and I have the *right* to go fishing Saturday morning" or "I won first place in the 10K race, and I have the *right* to receive the trophy." This is privilege, as a *right*, but it's what we can call "earned privilege." I have heard from many leaders over the years who will tell you that one of the main reasons for not being seen as having privilege is "I have *earned* (a *right*) everything I have!" Using a worldly lens, this reason can be justified within the context of the American Dream. However, can we, as followers of Christ, use that same argument? I would say, no.

First, the Bible is clear that everything belongs to God, not to us (see Psalm 89:11, Exodus 19:5b, Psalm 24:1, I Corinthians 10:26, to name a few). So, everything you possess is not yours, it belongs to God. Second, it is God who gives us the ability to acquire *his* possessions (Deuteronomy 8:18a, Hosea 2:8, I Samuel 2:7, to name a few). So, the ability you have to get up in the morning, drive to work, earn a paycheck, and return home has been given to you from God. So then, we can agree that any privileges we have *earned* are not based on what we did but come from God. So then, let's transition the conversation a little. To understand the concept of privilege from a racial context, we have to use a similar biblical framework.

Remember from Chapter 1, we saw in scripture that God created one race, the human race, and from that one race, all humankind was created. At the Tower of Babel, the human race was dispersed through the different ends of the world. We learned that because of the diverse climates, food choices, environments, and so forth, the human race looked slightly different in different regions due to these factors—that is, darker or lighter skin, facial structures, eye color, etc. Within that setting, let's fast-forward many centuries to the birth of the concept of race in the United States.

To establish and sustain power and control in the New World, early European immigrants created a system where anyone with white skin was synonymous with having access to social, economic, and political mobility. Anyone with dark skin (that is, Africans and Natives) was synonymous with denied access to social, economic, and political mobility and subsequently enslaved. So, from the beginning of the formation of the United States, the foundation of the nation was established for whites to benefit from these mobilities, which is referred to as *access*. As centuries have moved forward, whites still maintain control and power of social, economic, and political mobility. Therefore, being a part of the white race gives a person better access to these mobilities. Hence, the ideology and understanding of white privilege.

After attending a session that I led on understanding privilege, a white male asked if we could connect for coffee to further discuss the topic. He was particularly new to the concept of white privilege. He was an executive director of a large organization and was curious about how white privilege has affected his life. I was able to give him a deeper historical account and used real-world and personal experiences that helped him understand. He was distraught when he started realizing his own white privilege and how he has unconsciously participated in its perpetuation. We had a great discussion, to say the least. I immediately told him not to feel bad about it. He, like I, is a product of an unjust and sinful society, but God has placed us here in this country for a purpose.

After our discussion, he said he felt empowered by our discussion while admitting he had a lot to learn. He said to me, "I have to get you in front of my peers to teach them this. They have to hear this." Although this statement was flattering, I thought for a moment and realized this statement was problematic. I always welcome opportunities to conduct consultations and speaking engagements, but in this particular case, I wasn't the best person to have the conversation; it was him. I explained to him that one of the benefits of having white privilege is being able to gain access to spaces that marginalized individuals and people groups have more difficulties gaining access to. For both of our benefit, it would be more advantageous for him, rather than me, to tell his peers about his experiences with white privilege. He has more influence because he has the relationships and his story is powerful. After he and I discussed this further, he was excited to share his new, personal perspectives with friends and family to create change.

Kendall (2012) defines *white privilege* as an institutional set of benefits awarded to those who by race resemble the people who dominate positions of power in our institutions. The biggest benefit of white privileges is having greater access to power and resources than people of color have. Whiteness does not have one central and precise definition. It can be characterized as an ideology based on beliefs, values, and behaviors that leads to inequality or advantages rather than just skin color (Kivel, 1996), position of power (Frye, 1983), position of unconsciousness (McIntosh, 2010), and a universal understanding as if whiteness is based on what everything is measured by; thus, the idea of cultural racism is formed (Henry and Tator, 2006). Many scholars agree that whiteness is associated with institutionalized power and privileges; yet, it goes further and is best understood through its social construction and function in society (Chubbuck, 2004). With whiteness come assumed norms and behaviors, which are considered good; therefore, all other behaviors and values are thereby judged.

Pulido (2000) argued how white privilege represents a hegemonic form of racism, which has deep roots in ideologies and practices that reproduce white advantages. McIntosh (2015) has realized that white privilege is an "invisible package of unearned assets" that can be utilized every day. McIntosh goes on to say that for one to admit to the ideology of white privilege, one must also admit that meritocracy is a myth. Leonardo (2004) takes it a step further when he proposes that white supremacy makes white privilege possible. It is this idea of domination that allows white privilege to exist.

Leonardo (2004) goes onto to say, "Domination is a relation of power that subjects enter into and is forged in the historical process. It does not form out of random acts of hatred, although these are condemnable, but rather out of a patterned and enduring treatment of social groups" and "Domination means that the referents of discourse are particulars dressed up as universals, of the white race speaking for the human race" (p. 139). This domination by white America over black America (Loewen, 2008) is perhaps the most pervasive theme in the history of America. It is entrenched in the fabric of American society as we see it today and continues to affect our daily lives. Domination is different from dominance, as domination is a process and dominance is a state of being (Leonardo, 2004). Because domination can be traced to the roots of American civilization, we see today how dominance continues to permeate our society. Noblit (2015) explains that this white domination phenomenon goes far beyond whites who consciously or subconsciously act like the dominant group; therefore, they do not understand the impact their domination had and has on social relations in society.

This is particularly true in organizations where the focus is on providing a service to people, race, class, and gender (Collins and Barnes, 2014). Organizational privilege is influential for white men, especially in professions such as elementary teacher or social worker, where promotions and raises come faster than for minorities and women (Kolb, 2007). White male privilege is important to recognize due to systemic cultural norms, values, and ideologies. Collins and Barnes (2014) go on to state the following.

> Specifically, organizations that rely on funding and other resources from private donors often use strategies such as homophily and paths of least resistance to raise funds, gain influential volunteers, or access resources that otherwise may not be available to them. To gain credibility, organizations may also hire whites for positions that require contact with donors, board members (current and potential), and policymakers with whom they share common characteristics and social standing (e.g., race and class). In the process, they may intentionally and unintentionally perpetuate distorted ideologies associated with race, class, and gender and reinforce notions of white superiority, elitism, and male dominance (Feagin, 2010). Moreover, these mechanisms perpetuate white privilege, class privilege, male privilege, and the marginalization of employees of color and women (p. 63).

The culture of an organization indicates how well (or not well) leadership is attuned to race and cultural differences within the organization. Ironically, within organizations, most of the culture is more visible to those being served and frontline staff than to leaders. Lowe (2013) argues that to determine if an organization is "white," two of the following three criteria must be in place: first, the organizational culture is exclusive (predominantly white) as opposed to being diverse and inclusive; second, senior leadership and the board of directors are white and lacking diversity; and third, the way leaders process thoughts and behaviors typically comes from a white middle-class perspective that believes itself to be color blind.

Leaders marginalize people who challenge this norm and view them as antagonists. Leadership roles have been predominantly held by whites and supportive roles by black and brown people. Supportive roles historically include occupations that are physically demanding or of lower status or lower wages (Lowe, 2013). Keeping whites in leadership positions keeps whites in power and in control. Lewis (2004) takes from Connell's (1998) term and definition of "hegemonic masculinity" and argues "hegemonic whiteness" is the positioning of racial practices and meanings that firmly secures dominant positions of whites. This sentiment was also argued by Lipsitz (2006) when he said, "The power of whiteness depended not only on white hegemony over separate racialized groups, but also on manipulating racial outsiders to fight against one another, to compete with each other for white approval, and to seek the rewards and privileges of whiteness for themselves at the expense of other racialized populations" (p. 3).

The concepts of the American Dream and meritocracy are great illustrations of how whiteness influences our society in the construction, function, and application phases. The American Dream, which was coined by James Adams in 1931, is defined as a "dream of a land where life should be better and richer and fuller for every man, with opportunity for each according to his ability or achievement"

(p. 404). Hochschild (1995) identifies the four tenets, *who, what, how,* and *why,* of the American Dream.

- *Who* can pursue the American Dream? Everyone, regardless of race, ethnicity, gender, religious background, personal history, or beliefs.
- *What* does the pursuit consist of? Anticipation or hopefulness of success.
- *How* does one successfully pursue the dream? Through actions and hard work under one's own control.
- *Why* is the pursuit worthy of our fullest and deepest commitment? True success is a sign of true virtue.

These beliefs are deeply ingrained in the United States since its inception because of fundamental experiences of immigrants who fled Europe to escape hereditary aristocracies. The freedoms these immigrants felt justified to achieve were at the core of the rationale behind their deflection to the "new land." Now they were free to achieve success through their own merit.

The *how* is what is called meritocracy. The *Merriam-Webster* dictionary defines meritocracy as "a system in which the talented are chosen and moved ahead on the basis of their achievement." In other words, if someone works hard enough, he or she can achieve the American Dream. The big problem with the idea of meritocracy is that it implies that the opportunity to achieve the American Dream is based on an equitable and fair system. As we learned with whiteness, people of color have historically been denied access to social, economic, and political opportunities.

Whiteness is also perpetuated through the ideology of the savior mentality. The mindset here is that someone or something needs to be saved; therefore, a need is established in order for a "savior" to come and rescue. In a study conducted by Cann and McCloskey (2017), they found that whiteness was recentered through the framing of afterschool programming and a local historically white college (HWC) by viewing the community's youth as needing to be saved from their community and the tutors from HWC as the "models of success and guide to smartness." Here, whiteness was recentered by celebrating what these "saviors" had accomplished, but no consideration was given to see if these "saviors" were equipped to critically engage the students and community.

Having privileges over others is most often unseen by those with the privileges, in this case whites, especially when these privileges are granted based on one's skin color. Kendall (2012) compares this unseen privilege to fish asked to notice water and birds asked to notice air. It exists but goes unobserved because the subjects are immersed in it. Johnson (2006) argues that privilege is a culmination of the interactions among three forms of relational power dynamics that decides who is taken seriously, who receives attention, and who is accountable to whom and for what. Privilege is a power, and those who have privilege have control.

SYSTEMIC RACISM

White privilege inevitably leads to systemic racism. Before we explain what systemic racism is, we must first understand what it isn't. The biggest mistake most people make when trying to understand systemic racism is to exclaim, "I'm not a racist!" Whether that might or might not be true, we have to understand that they are talking about an individual, not systemic, level of racism. An individual level of racism is typically seen in one-to-one settings or is a person's view of others. This level of racism can also be seen in a group setting where one race directs their prejudices or discrimination against a race that is different than their own. That still remains at the individual level.

However, systemic racism can be conceptually and simply defined as racism within a system. In other words, it is systemic, "That is, it has been manifested in all major societal institutions. This oppression has long been a dialectical reality; while it has been an intense system of oppression" (Feagin, 2013). Another way to understand systemic racism is to understand what we discussed previously about the white race and subsequently the concept of whiteness. Whiteness means access to social, economic, and political opportunities. Therefore, the systems we all live within have been developed by whites and for the benefit of whites. A classic example of systemic racism is the concept of redlining.

Redlining began, supported by the federal government, in the 1930s, as banks would deny housing loans to blacks and other people of color based solely on their race, ethnicity, or where they lived in an effort to segregate the races into specific neighborhoods. Whites were able to purchase more desirable real estate in the suburbs, whereas blacks and other people of color were relegated to less desirable urban areas. This practice led to real estate agents, financial institutions, and other programs to geographically designate areas where whites, blacks, and other people of color should live.

Redlining is a term that has a literal meaning. Banks would draw red lines on a paper map to indicate the more desirable communities and would approve loans accordingly. (As a resource, Robert K. Nelson at the University of Richmond has collected actual maps used for redlining in "Mapping Inequality.") Zinzi Bailey, a social epidemiologist explained that redlining epitomizes systemic racism where "there was collusion between different systems—the removing of resources by financial systems, disinvestment by city governments, benign neglect, banks had to be involved, realtors" (Abdullah, 2020).

Systemic racism affords advantages to those considered white, because the systems that whites created are controlled and participated in by those they allow in and those they want to keep out, historically black and brown people groups. As Feagin (2004) notes, "Today systemic racism significantly shapes which socioracial groups have the best income, the best educational and economic opportunities, the best health, and even the longest lives." Systemic racism is invisible to those who participate in it but visual to those affected by it.

THE PROBLEM OF COLOR-BLIND RACISM

Another way whiteness prevails is through the practice of color-blind racism. Whites have depended on the ideology of color-blind racism to communicate their perspectives and ideas, and to explain interactions in regard to people of color (Bonilla-Silva, 2006).

The phrase *color-blind racism* alludes to individuals who do not "see" race. Color-blind racism has four central frames: *abstract liberalism*, which involves political and economic liberalism to explain racial matters; *naturalization*, which whites use to elucidate the race phenomenon by stating it was a natural cause; *cultural racism*, which uses cultural arguments to generalize minorities in society; and *minimization of racism*, which frames discrimination as a thing of the past and no longer affects minorities (Bonilla-Silva, 2006).

Abstract liberalism is correlated with political liberalism and economic liberalism in an abstract manner to explain racial matters. It's not races but economic reality that excludes some people from success, or so the argument goes. This frame uses concepts derived from liberalism such as meritocracy, equal opportunity, choice, and individuality. For example, equal opportunity was central to the civil rights movement, which was opposed by many whites. But whites today use the equal opportunity argument to speak against affirmative action policies because of supposed preferential treatment of certain groups (Bonilla-Silva, 2006).

Naturalization is a framework that permits whites to explain away racial phenomena by implying they are natural occurrences (Bonilla-Silva, 2006). Whites use this framework to explain that people like to be with others like themselves, and thus segregation is natural and their gravitation toward whiteness is almost biologically driven.

Cultural racism relies on culturally based arguments to explain the conditions of minorities in society (Bonilla-Silva, 2006). For example, "Blacks are drug dealers and criminals" or "Hispanics are rapists and illegals" are arguments used to explain the current supposed condition of minorities in this society.

Those who minimize racism suggest that discrimination and racism are not a central factor that affects the lives of minorities (Bonilla-Silva, 2006). Such statements as "It's better now than it was in the past" or "It's not the 1960s anymore" or accusing black and brown people of "playing the race card" are examples of the minimization of racism.

Color-blind racism undervalues the importance of race discussion and impedes efforts to debunk norms and the status quo. Davis, Gooden, and Micheaux (2015) explain, "When individuals are unwilling to identify themselves and others as raced individuals, they are also unwilling to recognize and address the disparate realities in which individuals exist. When racial realities are ignored, avenues for effecting positive social change are left unexplored" (p. 343). Beachum, Dentith, McCray, and Boyle (2008) also agree, stating, "Color blindness does not take into account the persistence and permanence of racism and tends to ignore or diminish the effects of racism that have resulted in great inequities in all aspects of everyday life for people of color" (p. 205). By ignoring discussions on race and inequalities, and recognizing and appreciating the cultural differences, the perpetuation of white privilege continues to plague leadership standards in areas of social justice, community development, education, and others. In regard to education, Davis, Gooden, and Micheaux (2015) conclude the following.

> Color blindness refutes the inequitable realities that individuals experience due in part to white privilege and race-based biases. Ignoring or denying these differences in the preparation of school leaders promotes and perpetuates color blindness as an approach to school leadership. This in turn results in the reproduction of school leaders who rebuff opportunities for their staff and faculty to expand their understanding of the educational landscape in which they are situated. Even worse, blindness to racial and cultural differences among students tends to support curricula and classroom experiences in which the cultures and experiences of individuals of color are at best minimized or marginalized, and at worst rejected and devalued (p. 344).

While this quote is directed toward the education sector, its principles are transferable across diverse sectors. Within our churches and Christian-based organizations, many leaders ignore or deny racial differences, thus perpetuating beliefs and views of the majority while neglecting the experiences of those who have been historically marginalized. The issue with color-blind racism in the church is that we simply minimize or neglect experiences of historically marginalized racial groups, thus devaluing their experiences that can be leveraged for the body of Christ.

THE PROBLEM OF ASSIMILATION

Assimilation might seem benign on the surface. Given that the dominant racial culture is white, wouldn't it be a good thing to focus our attention on assimilation as a way to eliminate racism? In reality, the drive to assimilation promotes racism in subtle ways.

Assimilation can be described as acts or policies that force those who are not like those in power to become more like them or to model themselves after the "norm" (Brayboy, Castagno, and Maughan, 2007). Therefore, the goal is for them to fit in, to become productive members of the system. Requiring assimilation, however, is a form of subjugation and power. For example, the US government during the 1800s crafted policies of assimilation to extinguish traditional Indian cultural identities.

A classic example of assimilation occurred in the 1892, when Captain Richard H. Pratt stated, "Kill the Indian, save the man." This speech was delivered in an address at George Mason University. His ideas, among many others, were to "civilize" the Indian; therefore, the development of boarding schools for Indians to "Americanize" them was developed. The goal was to make them "good Christian citizens." Within these schools, children were forced to cut their hair, and they were beaten if they spoke in their native language and forced to learn the "American" way of doing things.

Here are two examples of laws that were developed for the purposes of assimilation as it directly relates to Indians. The Indian Civilization Act in 1819 gave the US the authority to establish schools on

Indian lands to teach Indian children the American way and replace their known tribal practices with Christian practices. The establishment of the Bureau of Indian Affairs in 1824, which was under the control of the US War Department, was responsible for controlling funding for the assimilation and civilization of Indians into European-American society (Federal Acts and Assimilation Policies).

Though it's not so overt, the life-skills trainings and programs of many institutions today still push this flawed notion of assimilation. I once worked for a nonprofit organization that developed a life-skills program to teach youth in a majority Mexican community. When I asked what the purpose of the program was, I was informed that it was important to teach youth how to engage others and prepare them for work in the corporate world. Some of the skills that were to be taught were how to properly shake hands, use "proper" English, look someone directly in the eyes when speaking, and so forth. Pressing the issue, I asked what was wrong with the youth learning to use their own form of greeting. I was told, "That is not the way corporate America does it." This training program was specifically geared to assimilate Mexican youth into a "corporate" way of doing things while informing them in subtle yet profound ways about their own cultural practices.

In both these examples, we see how assimilation is telling a group that their cultural norms are not good enough compared with the norms established by the majority culture or race. Assimilation doesn't allow for the freedom of diverse experiences and culture to be expressed. It mitigates the concept of diversity by bringing everyone under subjection to a supposed norm. The body of Christ is built on the fabric of diversity: diverse gifts, talents, abilities, skills, and so forth. Assimilation kills the freedom to use diversity to glorify the kingdom of God.

CURSE OF CANAAN

One of the most widely held beliefs that was used to justify the classification and racial categorizing of blacks into slavery is the curse of Canaan. Canaan was one of the sons of Ham and the grandson of Noah. In Genesis 9:25 (NIV), Noah said, "Cursed be Canaan! The lowest of slaves will he be to his brothers." First, many people have traditionally called it the "curse of Ham," but as we just read, it's the curse of Canaan, not Ham. If Noah cursed Ham, then all of Ham's sons would be under the curse. In addition, Noah would not have cursed his son right after God just called him blessed.

Second, there is no evidence in the Bible that justifies that black people were the product of the curse of Canaan. The Bible rarely describes people by their color. For example, in the eighteenth and nineteenth centuries, it was assumed that the Ethiopian woman who married Moses was black, although the Bible never describes her color.

Third, present-day Canaan is located in a territory historically known as the Levant, which includes present-day Israel, Lebanon, Syria, Jordan, and Palestine, not Africa, where some believe that is where the descendants of Canaan were supposed to have settled. The connection of Noah's three sons to the three regions of the Old World—Japheth (Europe), Shem (Asia), and Ham (Africa)—was based on unfounded medieval associations during the first centuries (Haynes, 2002).

THE IMPACT OF HISTORIC RACISM ON THE CHURCH TODAY

Laws such as those enacted in 1662 and 1667 categorized people by skin color, creating an "in group" and an "out group." Being white and Christian meant access. Being African and non-Christian meant nonaccess. But these laws were made by people professing to be Christians and against the wishes of God. That they were able to convince themselves they were right to do so rests on a misunderstanding of who controls the resources in a Christian worldview. God controls the resources but gives humankind the ability to acquire and use the resources (see Deuteronomy 8:18) for kingdom work (see Matthew 25:14–30), which in turn provides access for others (see Matthew 25:34–41, Hebrews 13:16, and Proverbs 29:7).

God never intended for humankind to control access to resources using a system of racial profiling. Resources are to be shared, and all followers of Christ should be treated fairly and equitably regarding access. This kind of racism is the antithesis of what the Bible teaches. In Acts 2:44–47 (NIV), we read, "All the believers were together and had everything in common. They sold property and possessions to give to anyone who had need. Every day they continued to meet together in the temple courts. They broke bread in their homes and ate together with glad and sincere hearts, praising God and enjoying the favor of all the people."

In these scripture passages, we find God's heart toward the treatment of others regarding access.

- One—all believers had everything in common. Some of the things they had in common: their belief in Jesus Christ, their desire to share among the church, and their desire to build community. That made them brothers and sisters in Christ.
- Two—they all saw themselves as children of God, not children of what they possessed. They sold their possessions and goods and gave, not controlled, access to everyone.

- Three—they were kingdom focused, not earthly focused. They enjoyed the favor of all the people. They enjoyed what God was doing in everyone's life, not what everyone materially possessed.

Today, there is a plethora of research and data that confirms that whites still control the majority of the resources and access to those resources here in the United States. I'm not arguing that we need to strive for money, wealth, and resources; what I'm arguing is that controlling the opportunity to access resources is a systemic issue dating back to the arrival of the early Europeans and perpetuated today. Let me give you an example from my own experience. This is what systemic racism looks like.

In 2015, I was a part of a meeting with a majority of white Christian business leaders regarding their desire to provide and/or establish better economic opportunities and jobs for individuals within a specific historically marginalized community. These Christian leaders discussed potential solutions, such as providing job-skills training, motivational training, résumé and interview skills building, paid internships, and other workplace training resources and programs. While all of these sounds ideal, I couldn't help but notice what they were neglecting to discuss. The onus seemed to be that the individuals in the marginalized community were lacking the skills, trainings, and/or motivation for the jobs. While I'm not ruling out that being a possibility for some individuals, the Christian leaders neglected to look at their own practices within their organization that cause barriers for historically marginalized individuals.

I asked about their recruitment and retention practices—that is, where the jobs were being posted (if posted at all), what networking events they were inviting diverse people groups to, what leadership opportunities they had within the organizations that needed to be filled, what succession planning methods were being used to promote marginalized individuals to senior leadership positions, whether they were using blind recruitment practices, and so forth. What the leaders failed to understand was that access to certain information was controlled by their organizations regarding what positions certain individuals got hired for (especially leadership positions) or the criteria that human resource departments used to vet potential hires.

Research shows that hiring practices within leadership positions tend to be more symmetrical than asymmetrical. Leaders hire other leaders who think, act, behave, and look like them. Ultimately, leaders have to position themselves and their organizations to develop a diverse pool of candidates. Hiring, training, programs, and services for individuals within historically marginalized groups should also be accompanied by training within organizations to ensure equitable and fair access in recruitment and retention practices. When there are fair and equitable practices, historically marginalized individuals have the opportunity to compete for positions like everyone else.

PART TWO

HOW SYSTEMIC RACISM WORKS IN PRACTICE

CHAPTER 4

MY STORY: A PERSONAL PERSPECTIVE

Several years ago, during the hot summer month of June, I started my doctoral program. I was a little nervous, to say the least, as I was embarking on a journey that would be time consuming. My goal at that time was to develop a private or charter school that focused on youth in historically marginalized communities. One of the first classes I was taking that summer was Racism in US Schools and Society: Investigating Whiteness and Constructions of Race. (This class has since been removed from the doctoral program by the education department.) I remember sitting in class in anticipation, ready to begin my academic journey. In walked a middle-age white woman who set her belongings at the front of the classroom. I thought for sure that she was a student like myself, but I was mistaken. She was the professor.

She greeted everyone, and we all prepared to begin class. She introduced herself and, in her introduction, she mentioned that she was from Utah. "Utah!" I said to myself. I thought, *Is this some kind of joke? A white lady from Utah is going to teach us about race?* (I later told the professor my initial reaction, and to this day we laugh about it.) I soon found out that she's a nationally recognized expert in this field, has authored many books, and speaks at large conferences about her work in this field. One of the suggestions she gave our class was that the sooner we could figure out our dissertation topic, the better. She advised us that we could begin gathering our research regarding our topic during the course of the two-year academic program and use it in all of our coursework.

Based on what I was learning in that class, I began seeing my own experiences in a new light. I was able to attach terms and research to my experiences as a black man living in the United States. I felt an overwhelming, yet troubling, relief that my experiences were founded and based on a deliberate system of inequities that did not value my differences. This new epiphany opened my eyes. What really affected me was the dichotomy between what it meant to be a Christian in God's kingdom and a black man in the United States. I began seeing race from a different perspective.

I am a Christian man who is black as opposed to a black man who is a Christian. Just based on how this is phrased highlights a complex issue in the United States among Christians regarding race. My identity is in Christ, not in a human-created racial system. I started understanding my identity in Christ and the purpose he has laid out for me. That summer, as my knowledge drastically increased in the area of race and systemic barriers, I began seeing things around me with a new lens. I started questioning things I had been taught, organizational norms, how narratives were being told, and so forth.

During the same summer, in the month of August, I started a new job, working at a nonprofit organization that served a low-income, high-risk, black and brown community within Phoenix, Arizona.

Unbeknownst to me in the beginning, I was in the midst of cross-cultural challenges between the white leadership and the black and brown residents in South Phoenix. To be honest, I was a little naïve at first. I would be asked to do things in the community, like get residents to come out for events or get more kids enrolled in the after-school program. Many times, I felt like I was banging my head against the wall, because no matter what I did, I could not get residents to participate in events and programs. I felt like I was failing at my job, and I took it personally because I have always worked hard and exceeded expectations in everything I've done.

It was during this time that my life changed forever with understanding racial, socioeconomic, political, and social access and lack of access for different groups. The position I was hired for was a program manager that oversaw a Christian-based after-school program in a certain neighborhood in South Phoenix. At that time, I began recognizing that what I was learning in my coursework was actually being played out within the nonprofit organization. I began seeing clear disparities and inequalities within the nonprofit organization when it came to race.

The nonprofit was led by a majority of white, male board of directors and executive leadership team, while the participants, or "clients," they served were primarily black and brown. My position within the organization was unique, such that it allowed me the opportunity to sit in on the leadership meetings and hear what the leaders were saying, while also being close enough to the community they served and hear what the community members were saying. To my surprise, they were saying completely different things. For example, during the leadership meetings, the understanding was that the community was in need of our help. Without our intervention, the youth would have a slight chance to succeed. Another, more pertinent example was that decisions had to be made *for* the community because the understanding was that leadership knew what was best. On the contrary, when I spoke with people in the community, I was hearing a completely different story. They wanted to be involved in decision-making processes, and they felt disrespected, as "outsiders" were coming into their community telling them what to do.

After a short time, I began to reflect on the course Racism in US Schools and Society: Investigating Whiteness and Constructions of Race. I began personally experiencing racism, whiteness, white privilege, color-blind racism, and systemic racism from leadership and stakeholders. I experienced residents who were disengaged, angry, and outspoken (to me) regarding the nonprofit and its representatives. It wasn't a good situation for me because I began getting blamed from both sides. Leadership would blame me for not getting more families signed up for the events and programs, and the residents in the community blamed me for assimilating and aligning myself with the organization that didn't truly care to understand them.

There was a serious disconnect between the nonprofit and the community, with me right in the middle. For example, the needs I was hearing from the residents were not the same needs I was hearing in the leadership meetings. Leadership was saying "These kids in poverty need ..." or "The families don't have ...." On the contrary, the parents of the youth were saying their kids didn't need much of the help that nonprofit leadership was saying they needed.

I heard the neighborhood residents saying that they didn't want or need help. They said they were not these "poor black and brown people who need a white savior to come and rescue us" (quote taken from an interviewee). I was perplexed regarding what I was hearing from both sides. I didn't know what was going on. As the weeks and months rolled on, I began paying particular attention to what I was hearing, using the framework of what I had learned in my class over the summer.

Over time, my position within my own mind started changing. I worked for the nonprofit and represented the nonprofit, but I actually found myself siding with the community residents before siding with the company that was giving me a paycheck. I found myself getting frustrated in leadership meetings when I would try to communicate the experiences of black and brown residents, only to be shut down. As the only racial minority person on the leadership team, I felt alone when trying to plead with leadership about what initiatives to take when engaging black and brown residents based on the feedback I was given. On one such occasion, I actually requested to meet with my direct supervisor and the then-chief executive officer (CEO) and expressed the concerns of the community residents who had actually said leadership and the nonprofit stakeholders were racist. That meeting didn't go over too well, as I was subjected to hearing that I was wrong and the nonprofit was doing great things in the neighborhood.

After that meeting, I chose to stop speaking out on behalf of the community and assimilated to the organizational culture. But as I began to contemplate this new me who was assimilating to what I was being told, I quickly learned that if I didn't speak out, then who would? I felt like I was this black pawn dancing to the rhythm of whatever the leaders were telling me to do, to the point that some of the community members started referring to me as an Uncle Tom. I found myself in a place where I needed to either quit my job or stand up for myself and the people I was hired to represent. At a later point in my tenure with the organization, I was actually told from leadership that the reason I was hired was that they needed a black person in that position that the community would accept.

I began by strategically pushing back with some of the language that was being used in marketing materials, such as "poor youth, families in poverty, at-risk," simply because that was not an accurate depiction of the community; it was a generalization. I won and lost a few of these battles in conversations with leadership over time. This empowered me to continue speaking out and addressing areas of concern. I learned that it's not *what* you say; it's *how* you say it. Using this philosophy, I began using language that white leaders use but in a different context so they would understand.

One example was that I would always hear the word "help" in meetings and marketing materials. "We need to help these kids," or "We need to help these families learn," or "Your donation helps us help these kids in need." Based on that word *help* and the philosophy of the organization, I turned the word *help* into *save* when I would speak with white leadership. When they heard this word, they immediately defended their word choice by stating we weren't saving people but helping them. I pointed out that it means the same thing in this context. When they understood it to be the same, they stopped using the word *help* and changed it to *support* as their buzzword.

About a year-and-a-half into my position as program manager, the CEO of the nonprofit retired. My direct supervisor was promoted to assume the newly formed executive director position, and I was promoted to his former position, so my position changed within the nonprofit. I was now in charge of all operations for the organization, including staff, programs, human resources, and overall guidance of the organization. It was a bittersweet promotion for me. On one hand, a promotion meant an increase in salary and more responsibilities. On the other hand, I was taken away from the South Phoenix community that I had grown to love. After really thinking it through, I was reminded by a close friend that my new position would give me a larger platform and more opportunities to speak on behalf of black and brown residents within all the programs to whites on the board of directors and the executive director. The larger platform gave me the opportunity to discuss my experiences with leadership in hopes that they would give me the respect as an executive leader and listen to what I had to say and initiate change.

Unfortunately, it didn't turn out this way.

I now found myself entangled in a dark web of organizational philosophy and culture that was misguided yet fit perfectly within the idea of whiteness. The nonprofit used this philosophy and fell into the trap of not being open to hearing from the people who "need to be saved" because the leaders were the saviors and knew what was best for the people.

I had a few successes. In the South Phoenix program, we actually implemented a code-switching curriculum for the program. I was able to sway white leaders in understanding the importance of teaching the kids to operate in the white world while respecting and loving themselves for who they are. I also was able to make a little headway into how we view black and brown people in the communities we served.

I found out within the first year of working at the nonprofit that the book *A Framework for Understanding Poverty* by Ruby Payne was being used by leadership to teach volunteers and donors about poverty and its impact on the families the nonprofit served. I argued that the book was not based on scholarly research and was mostly opinionated and lacked substantial data. The book and the program to teach volunteers and donors were subsequently scratched, and we started learning how to appreciate people's culture through dialogue and understanding. Although I had a few successes, the majority of my efforts to bring about changes in the perception of people of color by the nonprofit failed.

One example of the latter was when the nonprofit sought to expand its services in other neighborhoods. The organization's mission was to work in lower-income neighborhoods, but they happened to be only black- and brown-majority neighborhoods. Instead of seeking collaboration and building relationships with those they sought to serve, the white-led organization decided what the neighborhood needed. I argued that instead of just utilizing an outsider's observation of the neighborhood to understand the residents in the neighborhood, we needed to understand the true needs of the residents by establishing relationships and building collaboration. A core, unstated belief within the organization, like many others I've researched or consulted with, was that leadership knew best what black and brown neighborhoods need. It is another example of this idea of the Manifest Destiny. This taking-over or dominance by white leadership reemphasizes and further establishes white dominance over black and brown people.

It was difficult to maintain my composure when I heard overt racist comments, microaggressions, classifications, stereotypes, etc. One such incident I remember definitively. I was participating in a tour of the nonprofit programs in South Phoenix with my supervisor, the CEO, and a couple of donors. We were updating them on the latest happenings of the program and our future plans—sort of like a briefing on how we were growing and having an impact on lives. We began discussing the work that the nonprofit was doing in the neighborhood and the transformative opportunities the park space could be utilized for.

As we talked and walked, we began unknowingly separating as a group, and I ended up walking with a gentleman and answering questions he had. It was apparent to me by the questions he began asking that he either knew something about this neighborhood firsthand or someone had told him about the black and brown makeup of the neighborhood. One of his questions was regarding an apartment complex at the end of the block, a government-subsidized apartment complex notoriously known by law enforcement and members of the community for having high crime, drug, and gang activity rates. However, it was a nice-looking gated apartment complex with a small area for kids to play, ample parking spaces, and a nice architectural design. It sat on the corner of a main street in the neighborhood bordered by a convenience store that many residents frequented. I was explaining to the gentleman that although there were high crime rates there, a few of the families in our program lived there, were engaged in their kids' lives, were wonderful members of the neighborhood, and were contributors to the beautiful park space we were standing in.

He stood there looking at me intently. With a puzzled look on his face, he asked me what was being done to deal with the negative behaviors within the apartment complex. I responded with enthusiasm that our nonprofit, along with several church groups, neighborhood groups, and law enforcement, were actively working to bring transformation to the apartment complex. Obviously not agreeing with my response, he said, "Well, in my opinion, those people in there are like cockroaches, and the best thing to do is tent the whole place and exterminate them all!"

My jaw dropped! I stopped walking and just stared at him in disbelief. I couldn't believe that came out of his mouth. I became so angry and told my supervisor what happened, and he excused me from the tour. The most troubling part was that this man was being introduced to the program to become a donor. I kept thinking that whoever invited him had to know his heart. I don't think he ever became a donor based on his comments, but I still experienced this form of racism, whether overt and implicit, a lot during my tenure with the nonprofit.

Some days I thought we were making great progress; then the next day, I felt we were right back to where we started. It was truly a struggle. Hearing from the black and brown staff and community residents in South Phoenix, almost on a daily basis, about how difficult it was for them to work with the nonprofit was troubling for me. It was almost like they wanted me to fix it. I tried my best, but this ebb and flow of emotions affected me greatly. There were many times I was ready to throw in the towel and find a new job, but then something good would happen and I would see the light at the end of the tunnel only to be left saddened by the mirage.

The few black and brown staff, some white staff, and some volunteers began leaving the organization when they realized that I was not able to make enough headway to bring about systemic change, through no fault of my own. The culture of the nonprofit was not conducive to minority staff and volunteers, and things started quickly deteriorating. For as long as I could, I shielded the minority staff and volunteers who had grown to respect me from much of the inequalities at the nonprofit, but I could no longer do that, as I quickly began getting worn out emotionally and mentally. I could no longer withhold the truth from them. I began being honest with them as they looked to me for guidance in the areas of racism and other issues. As they received the information over time, they began quitting. Some families that were close to the staff and volunteers began withdrawing the youth from the program. I began preparing myself to leave after concerning conversations with my supervisor and some board members regarding what was happening.

I learned a valuable lesson. Although you can present people with clear evidence of prejudices and systemic racism, they still will deny it to accomplish their own agendas. Their agendas and, more specifically, the donors who donated lots of money took precedence over people, especially in light of new knowledge of how privilege, whiteness, the white savior complex, assimilation, and systemic racism were brought to their attention. This was doubly troubling for me because it was a Christian organization. I could no longer be a part of this as my core values as a Christian were being challenged.

PART THREE

HOW THE CHRISTIAN CHURCH CAN ADDRESS RACISM AND LEARN TO WORK ACROSS CULTURES

Despite what some believe and others simply overlook, racism is alive and well in America. Worse than that, it's thriving in the church. The Bible has been used to defend and support slavery while being used to bring spiritual freedom to the lives of many. Christians have fought for slavery, and Christians have fought against slavery. The problem is there is no uniformity among Christians when it comes to dealing with racial injustices. Too many times I have sat in church services after a terrible, racial injustice surfaced in the country, only to have the pastor not even mention it, let alone pray about it. How are Christians supposed to unite around these types of injustices when two people sitting next to each other in church can't agree on how we are supposed to love all people?

Jesus says in Matthew 18:19 (NIV), "Again, truly I tell you that if two of you on earth agree about anything they ask for, it will be done for them by my Father in heaven." This scripture is often quoted, but I sometimes think, in the context of race, that two people cannot even agree on the most decisive and historically profound topic in the church. How can Christians lead others to Christ when Christians can't even come together on issues of race and unite their voices to confront, speak out, and work to change systems of oppression for their brothers and sisters in Christ? The early church in Acts 2 would have united and worked as a collaborative community empowered by the Holy Spirit to bring about systemic change.

On this particular issue, Christians all over the country must unite as one, as Christ calls us to do, and work toward creating opportunities where the kingdom of God can grow and thrive. Too long the church has allowed the devil to have a place in dividing Christians around a simple issue such as one's skin color being a determining factor of who's in and who's out.

In Chapter 6, I introduce a five-stage model that can be utilized to build cross-cultural collaboration and relationships. This model can be used within a one-to-one relationship or within organizations. The goal is to build God-honoring relationships and collaboration so Christians can appropriately reflect the kingdom of God while also instituting structures where all people groups can work to disable barriers and systems of oppression that block access to Christ.

CHAPTER 5

THE CHALLENGE OF CROSS-CULTURAL INTERACTIONS

The racial interactions between mostly white-led churches and other organizations and communities mostly comprised of people of color are at the forefront of relationship-building models when community programs or services are being offered.

First, let's define what culture is. Culture is a complex term to define. In 1952, Kroeber and Kluckhohn, American anthropologists, gathered and reviewed definitions and concepts of culture, and accumulated a list of 164 different definitions. Avruch (1998) provides the following excerpt on the ways the term *culture* has been deciphered. "In some idioms 'culture' is merely a label, a handy name for persons aggregated in some social, often national, sometimes ethnic, grouping" (p. 3).

For the purpose of this book, we will use Matsumoto's (1996) definition of culture: "the set of attitudes, values, beliefs, and behaviors shared by a group of people, but different for each individual, communicated from one generation to the next." This definition of culture shows how groups of people with shared values can become homogenous. This definition also conceptualizes understandings among many experts and establishes an understanding that helps us with our goal of building more successful cross-cultural collaboration and relationships within the body of Christ. This definition also helps us to understand how, when confronted with a different culture with different shared values, beliefs, and behaviors that are different from our own, we tend to view those as "less than" because their norms are different from ours.

According to Lebrón (2013), "Culture is an essential element in understanding how social systems change, because culture influences both the norms and values of such systems and the behavior of groups in their interactions within and across systems." Cultures then clash when one group uses supremacy to overpower, dominate, govern, and rule over the other. Because of this, barriers then produce communication issues, a lack of trust, one-way decision making, and racism that stand in the way of true transformative practices.

Due to the rich history of white supremacy in the United States, white leaders have made decisions largely that have benefited whites while disregarding equal, inclusive, and equitable access for other people of color. Martínez (2016) defines white supremacy as "an historically based, institutionally perpetuated system of exploitation and oppression of continents, nations, and peoples of color by white peoples and nations of the European continent, for the purpose of maintaining and defending a system of wealth, power, and privilege." The phrase "white supremacy" is troubling for most white people to swallow because it is also the phrase used to describe extremist groups, such as the Ku Klux Klan (KKK). Most whites are offended and upset if they are called white supremacists or considered to participate in white supremacy. While a person might not individually subscribe to white supremacist acts or extreme discrimination (for example, the KKK), whites have, whether consciously or subconsciously, participated in perpetuating white dominance over other races, which is a form of white supremacy.

Henry Grady, an 1800s American journalist and a prominent figure in the South, linked white supremacy and Anglo-Saxonism. He stated, "The Anglo-Saxon blood has dominated always and everywhere." Lord Charles Beresford (1900) stated, "The Anglo-Saxon has so far, chiefly owing to the mixture of blood in his veins, kept alive side by side both the military and the commercial spirit; and it is this unique combination of talents which offers the best hopes for the survival of the Anglo-Saxon as the fittest of humanity to defy the decaying process of time" (p. 806).

The doctrine of the Manifest Destiny, as mentioned in Chapter 2, is an example of white supremacy. In 1845, John O'Sullivan, editor for the *New York Morning News* and the *Democratic Review* is believed to have first coined the phrase. He used this phrase to criticize opposition for the seizure of Texas from Mexico: "The fulfillment of our manifest destiny to overspread the continent allotted by Providence for the free development of our yearly multiplying millions" (History.com). Vander Zanden (1959) sheds critical insight into three dominant mindsets of whites, decades after the Civil War, in relation to the issue of the inferiority of the Negro. The three major ideologies were as follows.

1. That the Negro was innately inferior to the white, and that while as a race Negroes might achieve a certain degree of

progress, still they could do so only under the pressure and guidance of the whites
2. While convinced of Negro inferiority, was less certain as to the "permanence" of this inferiority
3. Rejected the point of view that the Negro was an inferior or sought to skirt the issue as a major consideration

Out of these three ideologies, the first one was the dominant ideology by far within the United States. Vander Zanden argued that at least three elements contributed to the dominant ideology: Darwin's *Origin of Species* in 1859, biological differences in human characteristics and behavior, and Anglo-Saxonism, which is a product of modern nationalism and expansionism. This expansionism is the idea of the Manifest Destiny.

There are no questions that whites dominate and control the majority of the social, economic, and political institutions in the United States. Therefore, the decisions made by white leaders within organizations are based on a racial cultural lens that they are most familiar with—that is, the white cultural lens. Because the white racial culture is the norm, other racial cultures are seen as "less than," contributing to racial disparities.

Because they think of some groups as less than, churches and other organizations that collaborate with and/or serve people or communities of color take a deficit-thinking approach to helping these people groups. Valencia (2012) argued that this approach assumes that the individual fails to achieve success due to internal deficits or deficiencies, and these deficiencies are due to "alleged limited intellectual abilities, linguistic shortcoming, lack of motivation for learning, and immoral behavior" (p. 2f). In other words, the onus is on the individual to change, and not the system. There are six characteristics of deficit thinking that Valencia (2012) speaks to:

blaming the victim, oppression, pseudoscience, temporal changes, educability, and heterodoxy.

For the purpose of this book, let's take a closer look at the nonprofit sector as it relates to educability as it pertains to cross-cultural interactions between whites and people of color. Most, if not all, nonprofit organizations rely heavily on funding resources such as grants (foundations and/or government), individual donations or gifts, fees for goods/services, and/or fundraising, to name a few. Deficit-thinking philosophy is key to nonprofit success.

A book by Ruby Payne, *A Framework for Understanding Poverty*, is a classic example of how deficit thinking is perpetuated throughout our schools and communities of color. Bomer, Dworin, May, and Semingson (2008) reported that Payne's professional development programs are central to districts in thirty-eight states and nonprofit organizations nationwide, where many districts make her training mandatory for teachers who work in lower socioeconomic communities.

Payne does not use the term *deficit* in her book, but through the language, terms, and literature used, deficit perspectives can be applied (Bomer et al., 2008). Payne uses terms describing the poor as "violent," "lacking morals," "dysfunctionality," and "hidden rules" (Payne, 2005) and asks teachers in training to adopt negative stereotypes of "these students and families" in order to understand their behaviors. This similar model of thinking has led many nonprofits and policymakers to maintain white privilege in their decision-making, as stated by Bomer et al. (2008): "The book relies on a set of values—a framework—that exists outside of education, and is pervasive throughout middle-class US society ... indeed most of the American public, as it reveals the degree to which we use the education system to protect our own sense of entitlement to privilege" (p. 2526).

The field of education provides a good case in point, as does white-led leadership within nonprofits and for-profit organizations, where white teachers working within communities of color bring with them their own perspectives and privileges. For example, teachers are taught not to see race; to be color blind when working with youth. They reinforce ideologies of being racially neutral, which amounts to being racially blind, as opposed to challenging racist beliefs and deficit models in the schools (Yeo, 1997). Rousmaniere (2006) argues that white teachers not speaking about race is deeply rooted in the cultural and political makeup of the teaching profession. Rousmaniere goes on to state that silence is a weapon that white people use to ignore or deny claims by people of color. Ladson-Billings (1996) states that this silence is an "extension of their [whites'] power."

Pearl (1997) observes that deficit thinkers argue the need to receive funding to change the behaviors of those they serve. Valencia (2012) states that in social and behavioral sciences, there are four goals in regard to human behavior: to describe, explain, predict, and modify behavior. As deficit thinkers, nonprofit leaders are able to use this theory to describe deficiencies and limitations in certain individuals, families, and communities to communicate their purpose or mission to "help" others. Valencia goes on to state the following.

> Deficit thinking would posit a *prediction* of the maintenance and perpetuation of deficits, if intervention is not pursued. In sum, the three aspects of description, explanation and prediction of behavior are central to the way the deficit thinking model operates. It is also important to underscore that the fourth aim (modification or intervention) of the social and behavioral sciences regarding human behavior is integral to our

understanding of the functioning of the deficit thinking framework. This means that deficit thinking sometimes offers a *prescription* in its approach to dealing with people who are targeted populations for example, low-SES Puerto Ricans (p. 7).

This kind of deficit thinking leads to imbalanced relationships and an erosion of trust. White-led nonprofit organizations collaborating or providing services to people and communities of color must understand that there lies a negative relationship between racial heterogeneity and trust. Racial heterogeneity refers to multiple different races within a given population. When different races are present, different norms and ideologies exist. Race plays a significant factor within interracial trust because it is typically the primary way to socially categorize people, which shapes beliefs and perceptions.

In multiracial settings, Rudolph and Popp (2010) argue that the dissimilarity thesis, grounded in psychological understandings of categorization and belief compatibility, suggests that heterogeneity weakens social trust by heightening people's perceptions of dissimilarities between themselves and others. People who observe or collaborate with racial groups, more often than not, believe that those people not in their individual group hold different beliefs, interests, and values (Rahn et al., 2003). The dissimilarities between races play out in day-to-day interactions between different culture groups, and trust between groups is further weakened. White norms and practices are established as the standard of cultural capital, then perpetuated throughout society by which all others are judged.

According to Bourdieu and Passeron (1977), cultural capital is defined as the collection of skills, abilities, and knowledge that is inherited and possessed by privileged groups in society. Bourdieu (1986) expands this concept of cultural capital by focusing on the cultural resources that are valued by the dominant group. Yosso (2005) states the following.

> This interpretation of Bourdieu exposes white, middle class culture as the standard, and therefore all other forms and expressions of "culture" are judged in comparison to this "norm." In other words, cultural capital is not just inherited or possessed by the middle class, but rather it refers to an accumulation of specific forms of knowledge, skills and abilities that are *valued* by privileged groups in society (p. 76).

Bourdieu (1986) further argues that there are three states of cultural capital: *embodied, objectified,* and *institutionalized*. The *embodied state* is a skill or proficiency that a person bears or carries; the *objectified state* is an object obtained, such as paintings, instruments, books, etc., because the person holding these has the skill to use them; and the *institutionalized state* is a society with a formal education system that certifies an individual's competencies by awarding achievements—that is, a diploma, degree, or certificate.

The standard that is set by whites does not take into account the liberating capital possessed by nonprivileged groups and communities. By valuing this cultural capital, it can serve to empower people and communities of color (Liou et al., 2009). Montero (2009) explains how liberation, empowerment, and participation are intertwined.

> An important characteristic of participatory methods fostering liberation is related to the role power plays within its goals. Participation empowers the people and is also directed towards their conscientisation …

> its emancipative character is evidenced in its capacity to empower participants, strengthening their resources, and developing their ability to acquire new resources and redefine themselves as able citizens with rights and duties and the capacity to defend their achievements and demand what is due to them. It is also a democratizing instrument, as this type of collective action and reflection strengthens civil society (p. 76).

We must be careful of how we use the term *community*. I often have heard it used to collectively stereotype a group of people. Community can be defined as a social group whose residents reside in a specific location, share governance and resources, and sometimes have common cultural and historical traditions or practices. However, when a community is referred to as "the community," it can be a dangerous label. According to LeChasseur (2014), geographic conceptualizations of community can destroy the rich experiences within a given location. Warren (2005) argues, "For families raising children in the inner city, however, the quality of their lives and the opportunities and constraints they face are closely linked to residential location" (p. 168). Instead of focusing on deficits in certain communities, valuable resources and cultural capital should be embraced by outsiders (Perkins, Crim, Silberman, and Brown, 2001).

Communities that are mostly comprised of people of color have long dealt with issues of race and inequality. They historically have and continue to suffer from inequalities and inequities as a result of structural and systematic racism, economic differences, social dysfunction, and cultural domination by whites (Satterwhite and Teng, 2007). These communities, mostly made of African Americans and Latino families, were segregated and racially controlled by formal and informal practices according to Bolin, Grineski, and Collins

(2005). In their research of Phoenix, they reviewed newspaper clippings and correspondence dating to the late 1870s and found words describing black and brown communities as "dirt," "filth," "disease," and the "shame of Phoenix." These stigmas, along with intentional segregation, inequalities, and inequities, affect communities that are mostly comprised of people of color as they struggle to gain residential, employment, healthcare, educational, and social equality, to name a few.

It behooves us as a society and a church to break down these cultural barriers or at least find a way to build a bridge between cultures.

CHAPTER 6

BUILDING CROSS-CULTURAL COLLABORATION

It was during the first few months of my tenure working at the nonprofit that I had a meeting with my professor from Utah because I couldn't understand fully what was happening at work. After our conversation, she urged me to start researching how to better support both the nonprofit and the community from a racial framework. Based on what I found and didn't find, I decided to pursue a dissertation topic that looked at building collaboration, trust, and relationships across cultures.

Through my experiences at the nonprofit and many years of research that included countless interviews, focus groups, community forums, scholarly research, and much, much prayer, I developed a model and curriculum that serves to unite people from diverse backgrounds and cultures into building true collaboration and relationships. This is the bridge I spoke of in the last chapter. By following this model, you will begin a journey into steps to create transformative change in your life, your community, and your organizations and churches.

Today, one of the main questions I am asked by pastors and Christian leaders is, How do we connect cross-culturally and break down systems of racism and inequalities? It is important to note that developing cultural competencies for cross-cultural collaboration with the goal of being united is not a one-time practice. I would argue that developing cultural competencies has to be undertaken within your spiritual and leadership development journey.

In Ephesians 4:1–3 (NIV), Paul says, "As a prisoner for the Lord, then, I urge you to live a life worthy of the calling you have received. Be completely humble and gentle; be patient, bearing with one another in love. Make every effort to keep the unity of the Spirit through the bond of peace." Learning to love others is a lifelong journey. Love is the core attribute of God. That is why Jesus says, when asked what the greatest commandment was, loving God and loving people. Unfortunately, we never reach this utopia of love, and most of us understand that. But it's a lifelong journey that you must be intentional and dedicated to in order to continue becoming more like Christ. Loving others, especially those from different cultures, is particularly difficult when we don't understand the challenges, barriers, and oppression they endure.

We currently are living in more and more diverse communities, which means we are more often coming in contact with individuals and people groups who are different from us. Whether in our work, school, churches, or communities, we are given a great opportunity to build relationships cross-culturally. Churches and organizations are beginning to understand that we have to do things differently to reach diverse populations. One of my favorite scriptures is found in Revelation 7:9 (NIV). The Apostle John says, "After this I looked, and there before me was a great multitude that no one could count, from every nation, tribe, people and language standing before the throne and before the Lamb." Here we get a picture of a great multitude of diverse people groups standing united before the throne and Jesus. With my model, I hope to begin realizing this vision starting now on earth.

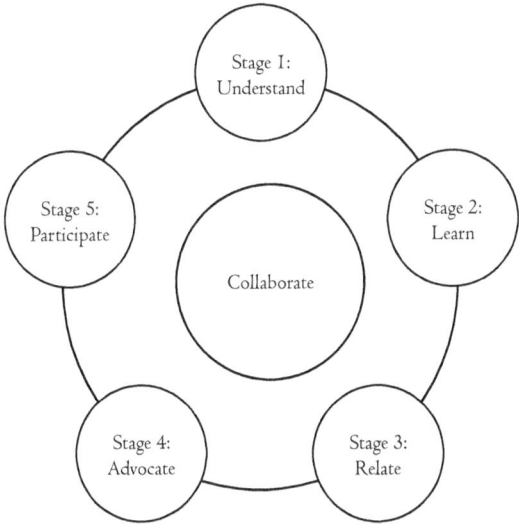

Figure I *Model for building cross-cultural collaboration and relationships.*

This model serves as a guide to build not only successful organizations but also successful lives. The model serves both leaders in organizations and individuals who want to learn how to build cross-cultural collaboration and relationships.

STAGE 1: UNDERSTAND YOURSELF

In this first stage of the model (Figure I), individuals need to assess their own Christian worldview, biases, decision-making processes, prejudices, privileges, and so on. This has to be the first step before any other step is undertaken. Why? If you don't have an honest understanding of yourself, you will waste your time trying to navigate through the other stages with your old way of thinking. Ayman and Korabik (2010) write, "If leaders are to be effective in a diverse society, they need to understand their own preferred style and behaviors and how these may differ from those preferred by others" (p. 157). Bonilla-Silva (2006) adds, "Being an anti-racist begins with understanding the institutional nature of racial matters and accepting that all actors in a racialized society are affected *materially* (receive benefits or disadvantages) and *ideologically* by the racial structure."

Self-Reflection

Self-reflection is paramount, but few of us do it. If our desire is to be Christ-like, then that requires constant self-assessment, reflection, and change. How are we to know our deficiencies unless we examine our ways with the guidance of the Holy Spirit? Second Corinthians 13:5 (NIV) says, "Examine yourselves to see whether you are in the faith; test yourselves. Do you not realize that Christ Jesus is in you—unless, of course, you fail the test?" To put it bluntly, if you fail the test, Christ Jesus is not in you! This is a scary, yet profound, scripture passage that calls us believers to examine our ways to ensure that Jesus is in us.

Understanding yourself begins with an examination of your Christian worldview. According to Porter, there are four sources that contribute to the formulation of a Christian worldview (Porter, 2013).

- The Bible—the central resource for all believers who possess a Christian worldview.

- Christian history and tradition—as the early church formed in the book of Acts, Christianity was carried throughout other places in the world, which engaged in a constant dialogue with what Christianity looks like within diverse cultures.
- Reason—we all hold beliefs, whether consciously or unconsciously, that sometimes contradict each other if we really take time to examine them.
- Experience—everyone has a worldview and it's affected by the culture, values, beliefs, and norms we form as we interact with others.

Given the depth and breadth of these sources, it is a difficult and never-ending job to learn how we think, how we make decisions, how we see ourselves and others, and so forth.

During many years of consulting and training, I have found this stage to be the hardest for people, and rightfully so. Being exposed to the realities that we didn't know existed within ourselves is a tough pill to swallow. We live in a society that doesn't place a value on critical-thinking skills yet tells us to believe what we see or hear. This starts in school. Horace Mann, known as the father of American public schooling, brought the Prussian model of education to America. This model was engineered by King Fredrick William I in 1716 with the goal of having children "depersonalized and isolated from each other at an early age. Seated in rows, they were easily silenced, controlled, and forced to engage in rote tasks whose sole purpose was to inculcate behavior" (Meshchaninov, 2012). Sound familiar? It should because that is how today's education format is 300+ years later! The point is that since preschool we have been trained to listen and obey versus developing rational-thinking skills. When it comes to building relationships across cultures, we use our worldview to inform us. However, we must understand that each of the four sources that contribute to our worldview has potential flaws.

The Bible, although we believe it is the inerrant and inspired word of God (2 Timothy 3:16), is interpreted differently by diverse cultures. The processes used are called exegesis, eisegesis, and hermeneutics. Exegesis, at its basic understanding, is the process of discovering what God was originally meaning through the author in a particular biblical passage. Eisegesis is how someone interprets the passages in the Bible using one's own created ideas. For example, the belief that the United States was birthed as a Christian nation was created by man and holds no biblical, historical, or factual evidence. Yet, many people believe this as such. Hermeneutics is simply discovering how the Bible applies to your personal life, situations, and generation. Here, you are utilizing the word of God to apply to a particular way that relates to what you need at a particular time, which is different for everyone. As you can probably imagine, just by developing a better understanding of these three interpretations, you can understand how different people and cultures derive different meanings from the same book, the Bible.

Christian history and tradition are also problematic in and of themselves. When you establish traditions, you breed institutionalization, which then births systems. This is what we call norms. At its most basic form, think about the church services you attend. Think of the unwritten and written norms of your church.

- Is there a certain dress code, meaning suits and dresses, or is it shorts and T-shirts?
- What is the length of the service? Is it one hour or three hours?
- What is the order of service? Is it praise and worship, offering, sermon, then close, or is it Sunday school, praise and

worship, announcements, children's choir selection, offering, more praise and worship, sermon, and then close?

The answers to these questions, along with many more, help us to understand the traditions or norms each church has and is representative of its culture.

What happens when a new Christian is choosing between different churches? They are prone to engage in a church that more closely aligns with their own experiences. That close alignment in beliefs and values helps perpetuate cultural norms within a church because what people perceive to be true is confirmed.

Reason is problematic due to our being aware of our unconscious beliefs and values. If we don't know why and how we make decisions, form opinions, and prioritize beliefs, then it's valid to say that we then would form contradictions within our own thinking. As Porter says, "many who hold to a worldview that endorses pleasure as a primary goal of life. They may not state it that explicitly, but they live their lives that way, engaging in all sorts of pleasurable activities, many of them to excess, to ensure that they get maximal pleasure" (Porter 2013). While they are indulged in a pleasure-seeking worldview, they might be discrediting their own health or relationships. Reasoning, then, skews their worldview simply because of their lack of understanding how they think.

Maya Angelou said, "You are the sum total of everything you've ever seen, heard, eaten, smelled, been told, forgot—it's all there." Experiences inform our decisions, which inform our behavior. Whether good or bad, the impact that experiences have on our lives is inevitable. Once, I attended an English-speaking church service, and during the service, one of the lead singers sang a verse in Spanish. It was beautiful and moving! Several days later, I became aware that some parishioners took offense at the singer singing in Spanish and contacted the church leadership in anger. My initial thought was not the ignorance of the people who called but the impact that had on the youth associated with these people. What message does that send to a young son or daughter or grandchild? The experience of that child is forever affected by the adult, which will inform, in a positive or negative way, that child's worldview.

One of the biggest, if not *the* biggest, influences is the media. As it pertains to race, for example, the media for centuries has cascaded a view of minority populations in the United States as poor, uneducated, problematic, troublemakers, criminals, majority welfare recipients, and so forth. As these messages are perpetuated day after day, week after week, month after month, year after year, what do you think that does to the worldview of someone? It's such a forceful medium that even minority groups believe that about themselves!

Unless we start asking ourselves the hard questions, critical questions, seeking counternarratives, uncovering the truth, along with much, much prayer and Bible readings, our worldview will remain unhealthy, and we won't be able to form a worldview that embraces all human beings.

As I alluded to before, I had to go through my own process of understanding myself, and continue to do so, in learning about my worldview, biases, stereotypes, prejudices, and so forth. I have learned through the years that I will never reach this utopia of understanding and I have to constantly work at it. No one is perfect, yet we strive to model our lives after Christ, who is our model of perfection.

During my journey, I began discovering purposeful acts where whites in leadership, dating back to the mid-1600s up until current times, created systems where people like myself were not included. To dig deep into the research was especially difficult for me, specifically within the church. I had to understand my own biases, stereotypes, and prejudices, and begin working on them. To be transparent,

I am still working on them and will always work on them. I will never be unbiased, but I will be more aware of my biases to help inform my decision-making processes.

That is why the work of the Holy Spirit is especially vital in helping us understand ourselves in this stage along with our view of who we are in Christ. In this way, the Holy Spirit counsels us, reveals God's wisdom to us, and convicts (makes us aware of) our sin and produces fruit.

The Holy Spirit is our counselor. In John 14:16–17 (NIV), Jesus says, "And I will ask the Father, and he will give you another advocate to help you and be with you forever—the Spirit of truth. The world cannot accept him, because it neither sees him nor knows him. But you know him, for he lives with you and will be in you." The work of the Holy Spirit is to provide wise counsel to the follower of Christ. The Holy Spirit is an advocator and reminder of Christ's teachings and the power that lies therein. It is through and by the Holy Spirit that we receive clarity of ourselves, the forgiveness we need, and the reminder of the teachings of Christ. To receive the counsel of the Holy Spirit, we must have a humble and teachable heart. If we are full of pride or we have a know-it-all attitude, he cannot do in us what needs to be done.

The Holy Spirit reveals God's wisdom in Ephesians 1:17–19 (NIV).

> I keep asking that the God of our Lord Jesus Christ, the glorious Father, may give you the Spirit of wisdom and revelation, so that you may know him better. I pray that the eyes of your heart may be enlightened in order that you may know the hope to which he has called you, the riches of his glorious inheritance in his holy people, and his incomparably great power for us who believe.

The work of the Holy Spirit is revealing. It opens our eyes to things so we may become informed to new knowledge, which leads to wisdom. This wisdom is to be used to grow in our walk with Christ and gives us power to fulfill our purpose that God has called us to. We can acquire wisdom in multiple ways. First and foremost, reading our Bible and meditating on God's Word is a great start, developing a network of believers to learn with and from (Proverbs 27:17: iron sharpens iron), and in James 1:5 (NIV), it states "If any of you lacks wisdom, you should ask God, who gives generously to all."

The Holy Spirit convicts our sins in Galatians 5:16–21 (NIV).

> So I say, walk by the Spirit, and you will not gratify the desires of the flesh. For the flesh desires what is contrary to the Spirit, and the Spirit what is contrary to the flesh. They are in conflict with each other, so that you are not to do whatever you want. But if you are led by the Spirit, you are not under the law. The acts of the flesh are obvious: sexual immorality, impurity and debauchery; idolatry and witchcraft; hatred, discord, jealousy, fits of rage, selfish ambition, dissensions, factions and envy; drunkenness, orgies, and the like. I warn you, as I did before, that those who live like this will not inherit the kingdom of God.

The Holy Spirit convicts followers of Christ in their life-long journey of sin, their flesh, and empowers us to live holy lives that produces fruit in Galatians 5:22–25 (NIV).

> But the fruit of the Spirit is love, joy, peace, forbearance, kindness, goodness, faithfulness, gentleness and

> self-control. Against such things there is no law. Those
> who belong to Christ Jesus have crucified the flesh with
> its passions and desires. Since we live by the Spirit, let
> us keep in step with the Spirit.

For the followers of Christ, the Understand stage is critically important as we strive to become more Christ-like. We cannot begin to change our hearts and minds without the infusion of the Holy Spirit, because the Holy Spirit helps us produce the fruit that is reflective of Christ. Scriptures are clear that our "struggle is not against flesh and blood, but against the rulers, against the authorities, against the powers of this dark world and against" (Ephesians 6:12, NIV). That is why when we are asked to change, are faced with new information, or open our hearts to receive new experiences, we cannot close ourselves off to the fact that God might be moving us into uncomfortable spaces.

It's important to utilize the Holy Spirit as your filtration system. Let the information you receive be filtered by the Holy Spirit so that the pieces you need take root and the pieces you don't need can be pulled out. If you close yourself off to new information as soon as you hear it, you are being the decision maker and not allowing the Holy Spirit to filter the information for you. I have a personal philosophy that I live by: No matter what someone tells me, no matter how off the wall it might seem, I never respond immediately, because I never know if the Holy Spirit can use just one thought or the entire dialogue to push me into deeper wisdom. I take it in, pray on it, and let the Holy Spirit do the job of filtering it. In this, I follow the example of Joshua.

Joshua was the newly appointed leader of the people of Israel after the death of Moses. During Moses's leadership, Joshua was his assistant and they both had different leadership roles to play in the birth of the nation of Israel. We can generally say that under Moses's leadership, he guided the Israelites from bondage to freedom from Egyptian captivity, established laws and commandments for the newly founded nation, and led them to the land that God had promised. Joshua's leadership role was different. He was to be the military leader, who would take the promised land and drive out its inhabitants to establish the nation. He did have military experience. Moses called on Joshua to lead a military campaign against the Amalekites (Exodus 17:8–16).

In his first military conquest as the newly appointed leader of the Israelites, Joshua was faced against the mighty fortress of Jericho. Based on his experience and the knowledge he had in combat, the way to destroy a stronghold like Jericho was to fight using spears and swords. Right? But look at the new information God told Joshua in Joshua 6:2–5.

> Then the LORD said to Joshua, "See, I have delivered Jericho into your hands, along with its king and its fighting men. March around the city once with all the armed men. Do this for six days. Have seven priests carry trumpets of rams' horns in front of the ark. On the seventh day, march around the city seven times, with the priests blowing the trumpets. When you hear them sound a long blast on the trumpets, have the whole army give a loud shout; then the wall of the city will collapse and the army will go up, everyone straight in."

Joshua received new information or a revelation that clearly went against everything he knew to be true. March around the city seven times, blown horns, and shout? What does that have to do with military expeditions? How easy would it have been to receive that new information and dismiss it because it was contrary to what he had known to be true? Yet, in the next verse, we learn that Joshua did as he was told. Point: God sometimes gives us new revelations that lead to new visions. If we cannot open our minds enough to receive new information, we will miss wonderful opportunities that God has for us.

Humility in understanding how we think, listen, learn, decipher, make decisions, and so forth is crucial to the first step in our growth. In Psalm 25:9 (ESV), we read, "He leads the humble in what is right, and teaches the humble his way." We have to be humble to understand ourselves. It's that simple.

Bias

Implicit bias is something we all possess. As I always say, "If you are breathing, you have bias." Implicit bias is the "attitudes or stereotypes that affect our understanding, actions and decisions in an unconscious manner" (Staats, Capatosto, Wright, and Contractor, 2015). Some statements regarding implicit bias according to Staats et al. (2015) are listed here.

- Implicit biases are activated involuntarily and beyond our awareness or intentional control.
- Implicit bias goes beyond stereotyping to include favorable or unfavorable evaluations toward groups of people.
- No one is a "bad" person for harboring implicit biases; these are normal human processes that occur on an unconscious level.

Implicit bias is caused because our brains are wired to form associations and generalizations due to the amount of information our brains take in constantly. Cherry (2020) argues that there are three tendencies that make us all exposed to bias.

First, our brain tends to seek out patterns. Our brain looks for patterns and associations in the world to store, process, and apply the information it receives about individuals and people groups. This is called social cognition.

Second, our brain has the tendency to simplify the world, which results in our forming implicit bias. Our brain takes mental shortcuts to process information to make it faster and easier to sort through the vast amount of information it receives.

Third, our implicit biases are directly affected by experiences. Experiences such as the way we were raised, our education, the media, cultural conditions, and so forth can contribute to the implicit associations we develop about individuals in other social groups. One of the biggest problems, specifically regarding race, is that implicit bias affects how we treat individuals from another race. We tend to favor our own ingroups and categorize outgroups in negative ways based on social and cultural conditioning. Recognizing and understanding our implicit biases is a lifelong journey that we all need to undertake if we are going to understand ourselves. It is not a one-time process to learn and understand our implicit biases. Here are some ways we can begin mitigating our implicit biases.

- *Complete implicit bias training* to help you reexamine your beliefs and associations with both your ingroups and outgroups and help make new associations.
- *Get connected* by challenging your existing beliefs through personal, individual relationships with individuals who are not culturally like you.

- *Use active listening and perspective taking* when engaging with others from a different culture. Always remember to seek (1) to understand and (2) to learn.
- *Challenge narratives and stereotypes* through awareness. Educating yourself on certain topics can help mitigate implicit bias. For example, some school districts have introduced antibias training as a part of their professional development to raise awareness.

The most powerful thing you can do is understand yourself. By developing a better understanding, you are setting yourself up for better success holistically. Paul said in Romans 12:3 (NIV), "Do not think of yourself more highly than you ought, but rather think of yourself with sober judgment." We have to develop daily practices that allow us to constantly check ourselves before we walk out the door every day. Paul said to the church at Corinth in 1 Corinthians 9:26–27 (NIV), "Therefore I do not run like someone running aimlessly; I do not fight like a boxer beating the air. No, I strike a blow to my body and make it my slave so that after I have preached to others, I myself will not be disqualified for the prize." What Paul was saying here is that followers of Christ must practice self-discipline by being aware of their desires of the flesh. We must focus on accomplishing our goals, and that means to crucify any desires that put us above God and others.

STAGE 2: LEARN ALL OVER AGAIN

In the second stage of the model, we learn about other cultures but not from a "savior perspective." After we have self-reflected and learned new, fresh perspectives of ourselves, we can open-mindedly learn about others. It is important to remind you that developing cultural competencies is a lifelong process. It's an ongoing, sometimes painful journey that we encounter but that can yield high rewards.

In this stage, we engage others who are different from us. You are thrust into intentional, unbiased learning, which can be a little intimidating at first. You are asked to remove stereotypes, prejudices, biases, and so forth as you engage others. The goal is to simply learn. You are curious. As my good friend and colleague Dr. Elicia Nademin (2019) said in her book, "Showing curiosity is about asking questions more than making statements." You're not there to judge, compare/contrast, or form decisions. The goal is to listen using active-listening skills, to watch interactions, and to observe communication styles. Watch for things such as nonverbal communication or how values, beliefs, and ideas are shared. The goal is to use critical-thinking skills and ask intriguing questions. Observe with the intent on learning. Let's take a look at two different perspectives.

In the field of anthropology, there are two perspectives of research, emic and etic. Emic research is from an insider's point of view. The observer most often places himself or herself within the culture of their study. They immerse themselves in the culture. They become part of the culture. An example of this is found in the 1999 movie *Instinct*, led by actors Cuba Gooding Jr. and Anthony Hopkins. Anthony Hopkins's character left society and lived in the jungle to learn about gorillas. He actually lived among them to the point that he was accepted as one of the gorillas. This movie, although in an extreme form, is an example of emic research. Immersion or some variation of it can produce a wealth of knowledge and understanding about a culture.

Etic learning, on the other hand, is what I call a "Google form of research." This is developing an understanding of a culture from the perspective of an outsider looking in. This observer would see culture without integrating himself or herself into the culture. While both perspectives have their pros and cons, I would argue that for the purpose of building cross-cultural relationships in the Learn stage, an emic approach is necessary. Doing life together with people requires an emic approach, but too often, pastors and leaders take more of an etic approach. My experiences with this approach derive from over ten years of working with Christian-based nonprofit and church leaders and teams.

The problem with solely using an etic approach is that typically we are viewing a culture from the lens of our privileges, worldviews, stereotypes, prejudices, and biases, making it difficult to truly learn. We then embrace a deficit-thinking approach, which looks at differences as a form of "less than." What this means is that we view other people based on what we know to be true. A great example of this is seen within the nonprofit sector.

I once used the following illustration at a workshop I was facilitating with foundation and nonprofit leaders. I argued that the majority of grant applications or stories about people are utilizing an etic approach to funding. They are gathering data using the "Google form of research" to inform them of what the needs are of a people group. The problem with solely using this form of research is twofold. First, you don't get an accurate account of the true needs, because they are based on what that person believes to be true. He or she is using a worldview that informs bias, which informs important decisions. That is why the first stage, Understanding, is extremely important. If you skip the first stage, you are basing everything on your opinion of how things should be based on your worldview.

I remember that many years ago I visited a rather large nonprofit with a few other nonprofit leaders. We were there because we wanted to see the amazing work the nonprofit was doing in the community. It was situated in the heart of a low-income, Mexican-American community. As our small group was waiting for the tour to begin, I couldn't help but hear a conversation between two leaders. They were discussing that if the nonprofit was doing such a great job, then why did the houses not look as good as they should?

I was standing right next to them, so I asked, "What should they look like?" They both proceeded to explain to me that if the nonprofit was doing such a great job, then the housing around the area should reflect that. As I paid closer attention to the housing, I noticed that it wasn't bad at all. All the houses were livable, with no major signs of immediate repair. There were a few homeowners working on their homes—that is, doing yardwork, fixing a roof, and so forth.

I started making small talk with the two nonprofit leaders, and I purposely asked them where they lived. Both of these leaders lived in a middle- to upper-class community that I was familiar with. What they had done implicitly was compare the houses they were used to with the houses we were seeing. Basically, from their perspective, the nonprofit wasn't doing a great job, because the houses in the community did not reflect what they considered to be a nice home.

This leads to the second problem with using this form of research. Solutions to issues or opportunities are based on experiences that we have learned throughout our lifetime that influence our worldviews. The key word here is *learned*. Here we are not as interested in asking *what* we learned; the bigger question is *how* we learned. How we learned to solve an issue or how we viewed the issue is not the same for every culture or racial group.

The Art of Loop Learning

Within the context of developing more culturally competent leaders, we train leaders about the concept of learning by using what is called loop learning. This concept of organizational learning was originally developed by Chris Argyris and Donald Schon (1974) but has been expanded since. I argue that the premise behind this type of learning is applicable and conducive to supporting changes in how we learn about different cultures. For the purpose of this book, we are going to take a brief look at three different loops of learning: single-loop learning, double-loop learning, and triple-loop learning.

Single-loop learning (following the rules) is the most common and easiest form of learning. Leaders within this learning framework ask the question, **Are we doing things right?** Many experts conclude that most organizations function at this level. They function within one approach. The conventional example used by many, including Argyris, is the concept of the thermostat. If you set the thermostat at sixty-eight degrees, it detects when the room gets cold and turns on the heat. When it detects that the room gets too hot, the thermostat shuts the heat off. The principle here is that there is little to no learning; it's automatic. It makes basic adaptations and takes actions based on set rules. Like the thermostat, this form of learning simply involves getting feedback and making the adjustment accordingly.

Within our context, single-loop learning is situational. Our behaviors are influenced by outcomes (see Figure 2). If an outcome needs to be fixed, we simply adapt our behaviors accordingly. At this basic level, our learning is predicated on whether the outcome is anticipated or met. It's what I have termed see-saw learning. When we reach the outcomes we expected, then, like the thermostat, we sit and wait for the outcome to change before we are moved again to respond.

The establishment of programs or services by a church in a community that is culturally different from the church that oversees the program illustrates this type of learning. The process typically goes as follows (in a simplified format): an etic approach to understanding the community is conducted to determine the needs of the community, then objectives are laid out, funding is secured, and then the program begins. As long as the expected outcomes are met, then the program or service continues. If objectives are not met, then leadership regroups, determines corrective action, then implements the changes to reach their goal.

Figure 2 *Single-loop learning*

The major flaw with this approach to learning about the culturally different community is that the rules are created solely from an outside-in approach and are based on the biases and worldviews of the "saviors." This type of learning does not confront our own biases and worldview; therefore, learning is limited. In a personal example, I started my consulting journey many years ago, and during working with my first couple of clients, I used to present information about white privilege to groups who consisted primarily of white individuals. I was expecting them to agree with me that we needed to work at reducing and eliminating it, but to my surprise, I was faced with pushback from some, if not many, people that racism and privilege didn't even exist. I was faced with anger and resentment from people for even mentioning it. I was dumbfounded.

My solution: a single-loop approach. I found and presented additional research and tools, and even started stating that I did my dissertation on this to convey that I knew what I was talking about. Again, this approach didn't accomplish the transformational change I was seeking for them. It did give people more to think about and created small incremental changes in their thinking. This is an example of single-loop learning. Henry Mintzberg (1994) stated, "Every manager has a mental model of the world in which he or she acts based on experience and knowledge. When a manager must make a decision, he or she thinks of behavior alternatives within their mental model." This is single-loop learning.

Double-loop learning (changing the rules) requires leaders to think on a deeper level about their biases and assumptions by seeking to learn new things in new ways. Leaders within this learning framework don't accept the rules as a given but constantly question them by asking the question, **Are we doing the right things?** Leaders are challenged to understand and redefine their assumptions, to think outside of the box, and to utilize creative and critical thinking approaches to learning.

Unfortunately, many leaders do not reach this level of learning. It has the potential of changing our perspectives of our view of the world. It's a higher form of leadership learning and supports the integration of new skills and data. Leaders learn and challenge their biases and assumptions, which informs their behaviors and produces the outcomes needed (see Figure 3). In times of rapid change and the growth, double-loop learning is crucial to the sustainability of organizations.

Argyris (1999) says the following about this type of learning.

> Single-loop learning is like a thermostat that learns when it is too hot or too cold and turns the heat on or off. The thermostat can perform this task because it can receive information (the temperature of the room) and take corrective action. Double-loop learning occurs when error is detected and corrected in ways that involve the modification of an organization's underlying norms, policies and objectives.

Using the example of the thermostat and the temperature in a room, heating and cooling are controlled by a set degree. With double-loop learning, the degree to which the thermostat is set is challenged and redefined by questioning if the temperature is appropriate for everyone in the room. In looking at an overall difference between single-loop and double-loop learning, Cartwright (2002) says, "They [managers] may be open to learning new methods or techniques that support their present management practices (i.e., single-loop learning), but they are likely to become defensive if questioned about the assumptions that lie beneath their current practices (double-loop learning)."

This statement reminds me of the scripture in Proverbs 1:7, "The fear of the Lord is the beginning of knowledge, **but fools despise wisdom and discipline**" (emphasis added). Leaders tend to learn based on their current knowledge and embrace learning that reaffirms their current beliefs and values. In double-loop learning, leaders are open to critically examining new forms and ways of doing things. They challenge norms, transform lives, and are rule changers simply by being open minded to grow in their leadership. Most leaders utilize single-loop learning. Double-loop learning usually doesn't take place until a crisis takes place (McLucas, 2003).

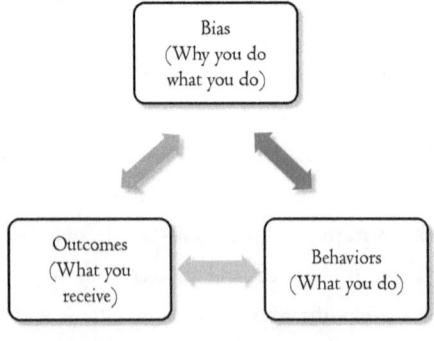

Figure 3 *Double-loop learning*

In our example of the Christian leader establishing a program or service in a community that is culturally different from the majority of the church's members, this person would challenge and analyze his or her biases before moving on to actions and outcomes. The leader would have a self-awareness about himself or herself to recognize how one's view of things would affect one's decision-making. The leader would be honest with himself of herself and others about their pitfalls and flush out any personal deep-rooted concerns. This leader would still establish the needs of the community but take the time to investigate his or her bias before springing into action, potentially producing a program more applicable to the needs of that community.

So, using the same personal example, I had to rethink my assumptions that most people are aware of white privilege. I had to talk with colleagues and peers of mine to help me uncover my unconscious bias, which was that people would be more open to learning something new and having healthy engaging discussions. I had to take responsibility for my attitude that I knew it all because I had done my dissertation on these topics.

Through these processes, I then redesigned the presentation on white privilege, gathered more impactful data and charts, and practiced my delivery and potential rebuttals. Now, did it work? Yes, people were more engaged and less defensive. They were able to digest what I was presenting on the topic and talk about ways to continue learning and growing in their lives. Although this was a win for me, it still wasn't enough. I felt like something else was missing, because participants would leave my training sessions with the information and that was it. It wasn't transformative. That leads us to the next phase.

Although double-loop learning is a broader and more complex approach to learning than single-loop, and most leaders would do well within this framework, triple-loop learning is where a few good, true leaders dare to venture.

Triple-loop learning (learning about learning) was not developed by Argyris and Schon, but the phrase does have points of reference in their work. This framework encompasses learning how to learn by examining how we learned in the first place. Leaders first need to understand their worldview and the context in which they work. This understanding allows leaders to frame how they make decisions and view the world around them. The context then informs their assumptions that informs their behavior, which produces objectives (see Figure 4). Triple-loop learning is transformational. Leaders within this learning framework ask the question, **How do we decide what is right?** I know this question is sensitive for Christians, as many people believe Godly values are at war with worldly values today. However, I would argue that while that is a valid and true concern, Godly values have been at war with worldly values since the beginning of time.

So, we must examine Godly values from a different lens than we are used too. Triple-loop learning can help provide some direction. Here, we are not questioning Godly values and principles, but we are questioning the context in which we learned them, how previous actions and decisions created the current conditions. To continue my personal example, I began listening and reading content related to white privilege and other topics, but my goal wasn't to acquire new knowledge; it was to learn how the material was being presented. More important, I needed to learn how people learned in order to move them toward transformative change.

To provide new learning opportunities for myself, I participated in webinars, conferences, events, presentations, and more. I considered the context in which the information was being delivered and had to understand my existing worldview. After doing this, I then gathered my notes and thoughts, and developed deliverable content to accomplish transformative change in people's lives. Although the ultimate decision is up to the individual to be transformed, I was doing my job to get the tools needed for transformative change to take place.

If there is one point that I want readers to take away from this book, it is understanding and utilizing triple-loop learning within the context of loving everyone based on biblical scripture (Mark 12:31).

This framework of learning is truly transformational, because it can be used to rebuild infrastructures that have historically caused division within Christian sectors and cultures. Regarding the manifestation of triple-loop learning, Romme and Van Witteloostuijn (1999) stated, "Members discover how they and their predecessors have facilitated or inhibited learning, and produce new structures and strategies." Paul directed us to think differently, to challenge our existing norms and values, and move onward with new ideas and perspectives in Christ. In Romans 12:2 (NIV), Paul said, "Do not conform to the pattern of this world but be transformed by the renewing of your mind. Then you will be able to test and approve what God's will is—his good, pleasing and perfect will." This scripture challenges a leader to not only engage in triple-loop learning but then to test it against God's will and have it approved according to his will!

There are two main learning sources where our worldview is developed at an early age: families/guardians and schools. Both entities are instrumental in forming the basic beliefs that many of us carry today. Although both are valuable sources, my hope is that we understand that both have flaws, as nothing is perfect. Because both have flaws, then we must conclude that our basic beliefs during these times need to be investigated. By reexamining our worldview, we question how we were taught and what we were taught, and in doing so, we can see things with fresh eyes.

Unfortunately, most leaders do not operate on this level, as they focus on perpetuating systems rather than "revisioning" them. I once worked for an organization that consistently used deficit language to describe its clients to funders and in its marketing materials. When I challenged leadership to change the way they spoke about its clients, they refused to change behaviors, and their reason was, "This is the way we've always done it." This type of learning level is the single-loop leader.

In the example of our nonprofit leader, instead of determining the needs of the community as an outsider, he or she would first develop a deeper understanding of his or her own worldview and bias to inform his or her learning. Next, learning about the community from both an emic and etic approach to determine needs would take place. Both forms take time but are extremely valuable in informing behaviors and outcomes. Why? Because what a leader might find is that while an afterschool program sounds great on paper, the deeper-rooted issues causing the need for a potential afterschool program

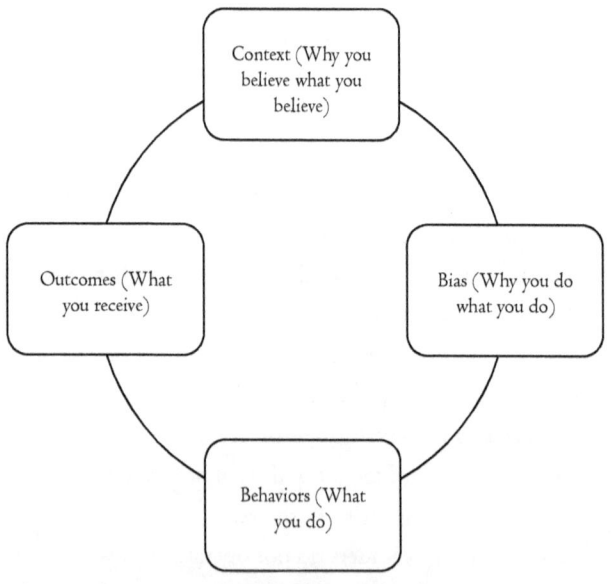

Figure 4 *Triple-loop learning*

are perhaps local governmental policies that cause inequities, the lack of better job opportunities for parents or caregivers within the community causing longer travel to and from work, or funding inequities within the school district. A triple-loop leader focuses on better understanding how to engage in environments, learning better ways of learning, and understanding how the organizations are making decisions. This leader is truly transformative in his or her approach.

In James 1:5 (NIV), it states, "If any of you lacks wisdom, you should ask God, who gives generously to all without finding fault, and it will be given to you." Solomon is known as the wisest person who ever lived. He asked God for wisdom so he could fulfill his purpose and discover new insights. In 1 Kings 3:9 (NIV), it says, "So give your servant a discerning heart to govern your people and to distinguish between right and wrong."

When Solomon made this request, he was a child about the age of twelve. As a child, he realized the importance of gaining knowledge and wisdom to distinguish between right and wrong. As leaders, we need to think with "childlike" openness in our prayers when seeking to gain new knowledge and wisdom. Jesus says in Matthew 18:3 (NIV), "And he said: 'Truly I tell you, unless you change and become like little children, you will never enter the kingdom of heaven.'"

At some point in our leadership journey, when did we stop seeking to gain new knowledge because we felt like we knew everything to do our roles effectively? We have gotten into a routine of viewing things through one lens and making key decisions based on what we already know instead of seeking new wisdom. Like young Solomon, we need to focus on gaining wisdom to discern between right and wrong. When issues like "How do we combat systemic racism in our organization?" or "How do we love our neighbor?" arise, we can seek God and others in gaining competencies needed to make the right decisions.

The triple-loop level of learning is key to creating transformational change for God's kingdom, but it can't be done without opening our hearts and minds to new information. We need to ask ourselves: How did we come by our current understanding of racism? How can we change that? Learning the true history of the United States as opposed to a romanticized version allows for a leader to better address systemic racism in the United States. Ask God to give you wisdom, and watch how it can transform lives and communities.

ALLY AND ALLYSHIP

Allyship is a word that most of us don't use often, as opposed to the root word *ally*. Ally is defined by the *Merriam-Webster* dictionary as "one that is associated with another as a helper: a person or group that provides assistance and support in an ongoing effort, activity, or struggle." It defines allyship as, "the state or condition of being an ally: supportive association with another person or group ... specifically: such association with the members of a marginalized or mistreated group to which one does not belong."

While both these definitions give us insight into the meanings most of us have learned in elementary or junior high school, we have to analyze their meanings within the Learning stage. One key component of allyship is the process of unlearning and relearning, which is a great illustration of triple-loop learning. Atcheson (2018) highlights three attributes to allyship.

I. A lifelong process of building relationships based on trust, consistency, and accountability with marginalized individuals and/or groups of people.

2. Not self-defined—work and efforts must be recognized by those you are seeking to ally with.
3. An opportunity to grow and learn about ourselves, while building confidence in others.

I would argue, from a biblical standpoint, that the second attribute doesn't align with scripture (see Colossians 3:23 and Matthew 6:3). However, it's important to understand the attributes as they have been originally laid out. Within the other two attributes, we see the importance of a lifelong endeavor of growing and learning. True allyship requires us to contemplate the context in which we learned what we learned. By critically examining context, we give ourselves better opportunities to grow and learn about ourselves and others.

STAGE 3: RELATE THROUGH TRUST

The third stage of the model is to Relate by building relationships. Building trust is the most foundational and essential point in this process. While this might sound elementary, it actually isn't for many leaders. The trusting framework I am referencing here is between diverse cultures, not homogenous cultures; also, the framework is your organization (that is, church, nonprofit, community group, life group, etc.), not one-to-one relationship building, although you can use this model for one-to-one relationship building. To put it another way, we can't walk into a trusting relationship without first addressing issues that perpetually break down trust. This is especially true in the United States, where race has been a template for patterns of inequality, inequities, oppression, and marginalization (Omi and Winant, 2014).

When I conducted my research several years ago to find the reasons why culturally different groups did not get along, I had to start from the beginning. For example, in Phoenix, Arizona, as in most, if not all, of the cities in the United States, racism was a major foundational tool. Extensive research and verifiable proof were conducted by researchers Bolin, Grineski, and Collins (2005), and they found that dehumanization and systematic racism were established upon the inception of the city of Phoenix dating back to the late 1800s.

In their research, they show how city ordinances and policies legally divided racial groups and established where black and Latino people groups could and could not live. White people lived north of the east-west railroad, and black and Latino people lived to the south. Public expenditures were used on water lines, sewage systems, paved roads, and other urban services in the north, while the black and Latino communities did not have these (Russell, 1986). The city's drainage and untreated sewage was directed from the white communities in the north to the black and Latino communities in the south (Mawn, 1979), thus causing horrific stench, disease, and filth. This continued well into the 1960s and 1970s, when laws were put in place to change discriminatory practices.

Now think about this: after centuries of inequalities, racism, and discrimination, when white-led groups are trying to build trusting relationships with black and Latino groups in this community, what do you think the response would be? I was teaching this lesson to a group of leaders, and one leader gave what I thought was the best analogy in response to this question. He said, "That's like me cheating on my wife for forty years, then coming to her confused on why she doesn't trust me."

Trust has to be earned, not learned. Gordon (2010) said, "Trust is built one day, one interaction at a time, and yet it can be lost in a moment because of one poor decision." Based on the research by me and others in our example of Phoenix, trust was never established, so how could relationships be built? To this day, in the year 2020, black and Latino people continue sharing the stories of their ancestors who lived in Phoenix and what happened to them. This highlights the lack of trust between cultural groups, and we have to revisit approaches to build trusting relationships. We have to be able to use a triple-loop-learning mind frame to learn about cultures that are different from ours if we are going to build trusting relationships. It starts by understanding the past, to better to understand the present, to build on for the future.

Historical Trauma

As stated previously, racism in the United States has historically marginalized people groups. Not only have these groups been excluded from equitable social, economic, and political opportunities; they have been the victims of such neglect and oppression. The purposeful victimization of marginalized groups throughout the centuries cannot go without serious ramifications to the marginalized. This is the concept of historical trauma. The word *trauma* comes from Greek origins and means *wound*.

Historical trauma was defined by Maria Yellow Horse Brave Heart, one of the pioneers in this field. She defines historical trauma as "Cumulative emotional and psychological wounding over the lifespan and across generations, emanating from massive group trauma." According to Mohatt, Thompson, Thai, and Tebes (2014), *historical trauma* was a term originally used to describe the experiences of Holocaust survivors (see Kellermann, 2001), but the term has also been described to represent other marginalized groups in the United States, such as Indigenous Natives, Mexicans, Mexican-Americans, Japanese-Americans, African-Americans, Palestinian youth, and many more cultural groups and communities that have experienced oppression, victimization, and other forms of massive group trauma (Baker and Gippenreiter, 1998; Campbell and Evans-Campbell, 2011; Daud, Skoglund, and Rydelius, 2005; Karenian et al., 2011; Sotero, 2006; Wexler, DiFluvio, and Burke, 2009). Wounds need healing, and to ignore wounds causes deeper issues and symptoms.

Historical does not necessarily mean in the past; the trauma is still affecting marginalized people groups today. I would argue that the mindset during historical events remains the same in some cases but has taken on different forms. To put this another way, think about when you go to the doctor for your annual checkup, a physical, or because you aren't feeling well. One of the first questions every doctor asks is, "Tell me about your family medical history, and have you had a related issue before?" To properly diagnose treatment, the doctor needs to have an accurate depiction of your history, both your immediate family's and your own.

A medical history is influential in prescribing the antidote needed for physical healing. It's the same thing with historical trauma. You have to understand the context of the history of a marginalized people group or community to collaborate on healing processes to bring about true, authentic relationships. Using my previous discussion about the research conducted in Phoenix, Arizona, as an example, learning about the impact of systemic and institutionalized racism and oppression toward marginalized people groups and communities gives leaders a deeper understanding of the trauma that individuals and people groups face.

Empathy

By empathizing with the marginalized, leaders can develop new knowledge to better build cross-cultural relationships. Connecting to others cross-culturally requires an understanding of historical trauma and events, oppression, and racism. Through empathy, we can begin feeling and emotionally connecting with others in our leadership journey. Dr. Brené Brown's RSA animated talk in 2013, "The Power of Empathy," highlights the difference between empathy and sympathy. *Empathy* is putting yourself in the shoes of someone else to understand their feelings and experiences; *sympathy* is feeling sorry for or having pity for someone who is experiencing hardships. She explains that empathy fuels connection; sympathy drives disconnection.

There are four attributes of empathy she references from Theresa Wiseman (1996).

- See the world as others see it (shift your perspective from yourself to the way they see it).
- Be nonjudgmental (don't judge others; use active listening skills).
- Understand another's feelings (recognize others' emotions by drawing connections to similar emotions you might have felt).
- Communicate the understanding (tell them that you can identify with their emotion).

Admittedly, it pains me to have to include this section in the model. I have always thought that because individuals are followers of Christ, we would treat people as Christ did. However, I have learned over the years that this is not always the case. The Bible is clear on the concept of loving your neighbor and leaves no room for misinterpretation. Jesus says out of all the commandments, the two most important commandments are to love God and love people (Mark 12:30–31). The word *commandment* simply means to obey a divine rule given by an authority. So, when Jesus says to love God and love our neighbor, if we are followers of him, then it's something we must do.

What does *love* mean when Jesus says to love God and your neighbor? If you look in *Merriam-Webster* or Dictionary.com, the first definition you see is love being described as a feeling of affection toward someone. The issue here is that many believe that this is the love Jesus is referring to, but it's not. The dictionary definition of love is affection; the biblical definition of love is sacrificial. "Loving others" is not just being a great person like volunteering time or resources to a person or community in need.

So, what is love? Jesus says in John 13:34 (NIV), "A new command I give you: Love one another. **As I have loved you**, so you must love one another" (emphasis added). Jesus was speaking to the disciples about his pending death on the cross. He was saying, "I am going to die for you because I love you." Jesus was not saying we have to die to prove our love for someone, although sometimes that happens. The love he means is the *willingness* to do for others. Love is empathy! For example, consider the following statements.

- You have the willingness to share in the emotions of others who face oppression.
- You are moved with deep concern for the kid getting bullied in your local schools.
- You actively listen to the pain of others who are affected by a policy or rule, instituted by an authority, that marginalizes a certain group of people.
- You experience deep horror when you hear family and friends using unpleasant language toward an individual or people group who is culturally different.

These are a few examples of what loving your neighbor could look like. In John 15:13–14 (NIV), Jesus says, "Greater love has no one than this, that he lay down his life for his friends. You are my friends if you do what I command." If we are to be friends of God, then our command from Jesus is to love one another, and if it means dying for someone, then that's what Jesus calls for us to do. When was the last time you were willing to go outside your comfort zone to love your neighbor who is culturally different from you? Culturally different, but united to the same race, the human race.

I am overwhelmingly saddened and heartbroken when I meditate on this question: If someone says they are a follower of Christ and does not love their neighbor, are they actually really followers of Christ? In 1 John 4:7–8 (NIV) it reads, "Dear friends, let us love one another, for love comes from God. Everyone who loves has been born of God and knows God. Whoever does not love does not know God, because God is love." This thought weighs heavily on me because I believe, as a collective church, we've missed the mark and are deceived in this area. How can people be prejudiced or discriminatory toward culturally different individuals or people groups and still claim they are followers of Christ?

According to my interpretation of 1 John 4:7–8, you can be one or the other. Either you love your neighbor, which is a sign that you love God, *or* you don't love your neighbor (prejudice, discriminatory, racist, etc.) and you don't love God. It's that simple! After discovering that God doesn't care about a person's race, ethnicity, culture, gender, etc., when it comes to receiving salvation, in Acts 10:34–35 (ESV) it reads, "So Peter opened his mouth and said: 'Truly I understand that God shows no partiality, but in every nation anyone who fears him and does what is right is acceptable to him.'"

As followers of Jesus, we have turned the act of "loving our neighbor" into one-time volunteer events or donations, then pat ourselves on the back because we did something nice. "Loving our neighbor" has turned into the pitfall that serving the needs of people who are different from us is equal to fulfilling the commandment. Now, I am not saying that it's wrong to serve the needs of others at all; the Bible tells us to do so. The point I'm making is that it can't be the **only** way we define what our understanding of loving our neighbor is. If that is how we define it, then we have truly missed the point. Here are some questions to reflect on.

- Americans have often identified the United States as a Christian nation, but do people love others as God commands and defines love?
- Does your church biblically love its neighbors? (How is empathy shown?)
- Do you build biblical, loving relationships with your neighbors, no matter what culture they are from, or do you just seek out relationships with people within your own culture?
- As a leader, are you seeking to hire only people for upper leadership or executive positions who think, look, and act like you, or are you practicing biblical love to all people groups by extending the same opportunities to them?
- As a leader, are you standing up in the face of the bully of hatred within your board meetings, leadership meetings, and organizations, and ushering in biblical love for the race of human beings?
- How can you use triple-loop learning to change the course of what love looks like within your organization?

Sometimes we have to answer the hard questions if we are going to grow in our spiritual journey and lead our organizations more effectively. If we are going to be leaders, then we have to get past superficial love and extend biblical love to grow the kingdom of God across all cultures.

Trust the Process of Trust

Once we understand historical trauma and have empathy for those undergoing pain and oppression, we can then work toward building trust and relationship—building trust through genuine relationship-building efforts. As Gordon (2010) said, it's one day or one event at a time. That is all it takes. "Trust is necessary to achieve positive collective outcomes," according Rahn, Yoon, Garet, Lipson, and Loflin (2003). A great way to start building trust is through the idea of counternarrative through storytelling.

To understand this fully, you must first understand what a dominant, or master, narrative is. A dominant narrative is a story or explanation that is told based on the interests and ideologies of the dominant group in society. A counternarrative, on the other hand, identifies individual or collective experiences that the dominant narrative suppresses or omits. For example, in more recent years, scrutiny about the celebration of Columbus Day has increased. When I was in elementary school, I remember being taught that Christopher Columbus discovered America and the celebrations we had.

The dominant narrative that was perpetuated through education was that Columbus was this awesome guy who discovered America and founded this land. The counternarrative explores reasons why celebrating Columbus is problematic—that is, extreme violence toward the indigenous people who were already in the New World, the fact that you cannot discover something that wasn't lost, the establishment of the transatlantic slave trade, and the multiple deadly diseases that Columbus and his crew brought with them to the New World.

Bamberg (2004) argued that the dominant narratives serve as a roadmap, and this roadmap serves to "normalize" and "naturalize" events, which restricts how behavior and accounts are utilized. Bamberg and Andrew (2004) focused research on using individual stories as a counternarrative to discuss commonalities with a society. I argue that having a healthy balance of dominant and counternarratives can be highly impactful in relationship-building efforts. Again, if we revisit our idea of triple-loop learning, a group could understand what the dominant narrative is, unpack the counternarrative, and develop new understandings through a collaborative process, which would result in some form of commonality.

How we understand people's stories and views helps build trust across cultures. We are connected through commonalities. Commonalities bridge gaps in our cultural differences. This is why the first two stages in the model are critically important to process and put into practice. To fully understand someone else's story, you must know your biases and worldview, because that influences how you perceive the information you are getting. You have to learn about others through etic and emic processes to see their cultures as different from, but still equal in value to, yours. Building cross-cultural relationships requires intentionality.

Building trust within human relationships is foundational and fundamental: no trust, no relationship. However, this doesn't mean we need to trust anyone and everyone. Scripture tells us: It's better to trust in God than in man (Psalm 118:8); Do not walk in the ways of the wicked, stand in the way of sinners and sit in the company of mockers (Psalm 1:1); Stay away from angry people (Proverbs 22:24–25); All human beings are sinful (Romans 3:23); and We are among wolves (Matthew 10:16). That doesn't make us forget our command to love another (Mark 12:31); walk with the wise (Proverbs 13:20); iron sharpens iron (Proverbs 27:17); doing life with others (Ecclesiastes 4:9–12); and speaking the truth to each other in love (Ephesians 4:15).

It is important to note that building cross-cultural relationships will take time. It's not that once we accomplish it, we can say "Done" and move on. It's going to take months or even years to build true, authentic trust across cultures. Trust involves being transparent and honest with ourselves and others. Because we can control only ourselves, focusing our efforts on being a person with high character, morals, and Godly values will attract the like. Moving on to the next step in the model should be done with the understanding that trust building is ongoing. As new opportunities and issues arise, relationships are constantly tested, and trust has to be revisited on an ongoing basis.

STAGE 4: ADVOCATE FOR A CAUSE

Only after we build trust and create relationships, can we better support the other group in the form of true advocacy. We have learned in all these stages that we are continually growing and developing ourselves, our organizations, and our staff. This model is not a one-time learning process but a lifetime cycle of learning we must embrace.

In the Understand stage of the model, we learned that we need to conduct a thorough self-awareness assessment. We need to check our Christian worldview, biases, prejudices, stereotypes, decision-making processes, and so forth.

In the Learn stage, we are developing ways to learn through both emic and etic processes and engaging in loop learning. We are considering how our organization processes information regarding those from different cultures. We are setting ourselves up to learn information we've never heard before, because we are building our understandings of ourselves and others.

The Relate stage enables us to build authentic relationships with diverse cultural groups. Trust is the most important component. Without it, we will never have the relationships that God intends for us to have with all brothers and sisters in Christ. To understand how trust is built, we need to engage in conversations about historical trauma through an empathetic heart. Empathy carries weight in building trust.

In the Advocate stage, we are motivated through compassion. The Bible is full of examples of advocacy work from Genesis to Revelation. The Bible says that Jesus is our advocate. In 1 John 2:1 (NIV), "My dear children, I write this to you so that you will not sin. But if anybody does sin, we have an advocate with the Father—Jesus Christ, the Righteous One." In other portions of scripture, Jesus says the Holy Spirit is our advocate (John 14:16, 26; 15:26; 16:7).

Think about our justice system, where attorneys can be considered our legal advocates who speak on behalf of their clients. The word *advocate* comes from the Greek word *parakleton*, which means helper, counselor, and advisor. As Jesus and the Holy Spirit are our advocates, we too are called to advocate for others. Let's look at a few scriptures (emphasis added) from the Bible (NIV) regarding advocacy.

- Galatians 6:2—"**Carry** each other's burdens, and in this way you will fulfill the law of Christ."
- Proverbs 31:8–9—"**Speak up** for those who cannot speak for themselves, for the rights of all who are destitute.

Speak up and judge fairly; **defend** the rights of the poor and needy."
- Psalm 82:3—"**Defend** the weak and the fatherless; **uphold** the cause of the poor and oppressed."
- Zechariah 7:9—"This is what the Lord Almighty said: '**Administer** true justice; **show** mercy and compassion to one another.'"
- Proverbs 29:7—"The righteous **care** about justice for the poor, but the wicked have no such concern."

I want to focus your attention on the words in bold, which are verbs. Verbs in these scriptures constitute an action or doing. *Carry* burdens. *Speak up. Administer*, and so forth. Advocacy is not a choice, but a command based on scripture. We must be involved with some actionable process that is seeking justice for the oppressed, the weak, the poor, etc. As I mentioned earlier, donating food to the poor or volunteering at an event are wonderful things, but they are not advocacy.

Advocacy is working for a cause or issue to bring about change for a person or a community. The type of advocacy that the Bible talks about is clear: collective advocacy, not self-advocacy. Self-advocacy is an individual speaking up for himself or herself; collective advocacy involves a group, a community, or a church. In the scriptures we just read, the call is for believers in Christ to unite to advocate on the behalf of those oppressed or marginalized in society.

Advocacy seeks to empower Christian leaders in leading their organizations in collaborating with those oppressed and marginalized by advocating on issues relevant to them. Through the understanding, learning, and relationship-building stages, we now are able to address the real needs, not perceived needs. The real needs are identified in the Learn and Relate stages of the process. An interesting point of reference within the education field, Khalifa (2015) states, "Advocating for community-based interests and causes that may have nothing at all to do with schools or education can be deeply advantageous for educators." While I agree with this statement, within the context of the Christian leaders I would change it to state, "Advocating for community-based interests and causes has everything to do with churches and Christian-based organizations and can be deeply advantageous for followers of Christ." The goal of advocating is not for Christianity as an institution, but Christianity as Christ's body. How do we advocate? Simple: we must advocate through compassion.

Compassion

We saw how empathy is critically important in building cross-cultural relationships. While empathy is good for that stage, compassion is needed for advocacy. Compassion, in the Christian sense, builds on empathy. Empathy feels; compassion moves. See the difference between the two as illustrated by these examples.

- **Empathy:** You have the willingness to share in the emotions of others who face oppression.
- **Compassion:** You engage in dismantling systems of oppression that others face by actively holding leadership accountable to create equitable systems.
- **Empathy:** You are moved with deep concern for the kid getting bullied in your local schools.
- **Compassion:** You speak with school administrators to inform them of the student being bullied so the bullies are identified and held accountable.

- **Empathy:** You actively listen to the pain of others who are affected by a policy or rule instituted by an authority that marginalizes a certain group of people.
- **Compassion:** You participate in community forums or board meetings to address your concerns for the marginalized group and fight for fair policymaking for everyone.
- **Empathy:** You experience deep horror when you hear family and friends using unpleasant language toward an individual or people group who is culturally different.
- **Compassion:** You confront your family and friends who use unpleasant language toward a culturally different individual or people group by asking them not to speak like that.

Compassion is actually walking alongside others in the face of their opposition. It's taking action on behalf of the kid getting bullied at school. You are feeling the pain of a policy or rule instituted by an authority that marginalizes a certain group of people as you stand side by side with your brother or sister in Christ, and you are moved to speak out against it. It's the willingness to share in the suffering of your neighbors who have lost everything and gathering resources to help them rebuild. It's imagining yourself fighting in the shoes of marginalized people groups about how inequities within social, economic, and political sectors affect their lives and voting to change initiatives. It's the horror you feel when peers and friends use unpleasant language toward an individual or people group who is culturally different and speaking up for those without a voice. Do you see the slight variation? Compassion is love in action! Compassion is empathy in motion. Look carefully at this scripture passage (Matthew 9:35–38 NIV) of Jesus's ministry to highlight this.

> Jesus went through all the towns and villages, teaching in their synagogues, proclaiming the good news of the kingdom and healing every disease and sickness. When he saw the crowds, he had compassion on them, because they were harassed and helpless, like a sheep without a shepherd. Then he said to his disciples, "The harvest is plentiful but the workers are few. Ask the Lord of the harvest, therefore, to send out workers into his harvest field."

There is a lot in this passage to unpack, but I want to focus on what we learned about empathy and compassion. Do you see where Jesus has empathy? Now, do you see where he has compassion? Jesus has empathy when he saw how the crowds were harassed and helpless. (Think about today's marginalized people whom we've been discussing, who don't have a voice.) Jesus had compassion when he said, "Ask the Lord." Remember that empathy is feeling (crowds are harassed and helpless), so Jesus felt something for them, and compassion is action (Ask the Lord). Compassion builds from empathy.

Let's look at another passage from Matthew 15:30–39 (NIV).

> Great crowds came to him, bringing the lame, the blind, the crippled, the mute and many others, and laid them at his feet; and he healed them. The people were amazed when they saw the mute speaking, the crippled made well, the lame walking and the blind seeing. And they praised the God of Israel. Jesus called his disciples to him and said, "I have compassion for these people; they have already been with me three days and have nothing to eat. I do not want to send them away hungry, or they may collapse on the way." His disciples

> answered, "Where could we get enough bread in this remote place to feed such a crowd?" "How many loaves do you have?" Jesus asked. "Seven," they replied, "and a few small fish." He told the crowd to sit down on the ground. Then he took the seven loaves and the fish, and when he had given thanks, he broke them and gave them to the disciples, and they in turn to the people. They all ate and were satisfied. Afterward the disciples picked up seven basketfuls of broken pieces that were left over. The number of those who ate was four thousand men, besides women and children. After Jesus had sent the crowd away, he got into the boat and went to the vicinity of Magadan.

Let's do the same exercise. Do you see where Jesus has empathy? Now, do you see where he has compassion? Jesus showed empathy by understanding that people have been with him for three days and have had nothing to eat. He felt they were tired and hungry. Therefore, he had compassion by serving them lunch. One more example in the Parable of the Lost Son from Luke 15:11–32 (NIV).

> Jesus continued: "There was a man who had two sons. The younger one said to his father, 'Father, give me my share of the estate.' So, he divided his property between them. Not long after that, the younger son got together all he had, set off for a distant country and there squandered his wealth in wild living.
>
> After he had spent everything, there was a severe famine in that whole country, and he began to be in need .... I will set out and go back to my father and say to him: 'Father, I have sinned against heaven and against

you. I am no longer worthy to be called your son; make me like one of your hired servants.' So he got up and went to his father.

But while he was still a long way off, his father saw him and was filled with compassion for him; he ran to his son, threw his arms around him and kissed him. 'Let's have a feast and celebrate. For this son of mine was dead and is alive again; he was lost and is found.'

Meanwhile, the older son was in the field. When he came near the house, he heard music and dancing. So he called one of the servants and asked him what was going on. 'Your brother has come,' he replied, 'and your father has killed the fattened calf because he has him back safe and sound.' The older brother became angry and refused to go in.

So, his father went out and pleaded with him. But he answered his father, 'Look! All these years I've been slaving for you and never disobeyed your orders. Yet you never gave me even a young goat so I could celebrate with my friends. But when this son of yours who has squandered your property with prostitutes comes home, you kill the fattened calf for him!'

'My son,' the father said, 'you are always with me, and everything I have is yours. But we had to celebrate and be glad, because this brother of yours was dead and is alive again; he was lost and is found" (Luke 15:11–32).

This one is a little bit trickier. Do you see empathy? Now, do you see compassion? Think of the context of this parable. Jesus is sitting with tax collectors and sinners as the Pharisees and teachers of the law are critical of Jesus for eating with *that* type of people. In the parable of the lost son, empathy is shown by the son's father (who represents God), who understands the harsh plight we take when not following after him. He understands the hardships we face while we are in sin, but his compassion lies in the forgiveness of our sins. Like the father in the parable, God welcomes us home with open arms, and we are celebrated because we were lost and now we are found.

Most leaders when reading this might argue that their church or nonprofit is doing something to help those marginalized. For example, church members might be empathetic and see the need in their community to feed the hungry; then they are moved with compassion to provide food pantries or deliver food to those in need. A nonprofit staff might be empathetic and see a need to serve youth and move with compassion to start a recreation league. These are great initiatives, but advocacy work is deeper. Advocacy work changes systems. Advocacy work changes institutions.

The concept of being an advocacy leader must operate on three levels: the individual level, the systemic level, and the broader level (Anderson, 2009). I would argue that most leaders strive to operate on the *individual* level, which advocates on behalf of a person. In using our previous example of the nonprofit leader and the after-school program, the nonprofit leader would be focused only on providing resources to help the child read, provide a meal, or assist with homework. This level advocacy is definitely needed but can't be an absolute, year in and year out. At some point, the leader would need to grow in his or her leadership development and recognize that bigger systems are at play.

The *systemic* level of advocacy seeks to dismantle issues that are perpetuated within the systems that cause this child, for example, to lack reading skills, meals, or homework assistance. Within the scope of his or her organization, this leader would include strategies about attending school district board meetings, visiting school principals, talking to teachers, and collaborating with parents or caregivers. A systemic-minded advocacy leader would seek to understand the whys and hows of the system, the root causes, the gaps, etc. (Think triple-loop.)

A *broader*-level leader sees inequities at a higher level and understands that things might not be within his or her scope to change. By understanding this, the leader builds strategies to create learning opportunities for the youth in the afterschool program to become change agents and leaders for the next generation, as he or she can help influence policies.

As followers of Christ, a leader must operate on all three levels, but he or she can't just stay at the individual level. He or she, at some point, must spend the majority of their advocacy work within the systemic and broader levels, where he or she has influence and power to create change. These are the *Carry* burdens—*Speak up, Administer,* and so forth—that scripture tells us to do.

There are two great illustrations of the different levels of advocacy in the Bible. The first is found in Acts 6:1–6 (NLT).

> But as the believers rapidly multiplied, there were rumblings of discontent. The Greek-speaking believers complained about the Hebrew-speaking believers, saying that their widows were being discriminated against in the daily distribution of food. So the Twelve called a meeting of all the believers. They said, "We apostles should spend our time teaching the word of God, not running a food program. And so, brothers, select seven men who are well respected and are full of the Spirit and wisdom. We will give them this responsibility.

> Then we apostles can spend our time in prayer and teaching the word." Everyone liked this idea, and they chose the following: Stephen (a man full of faith and the Holy Spirit), Philip, Procorus, Nicanor, Timon, Parmenas, and Nicolas of Antioch (an earlier convert to the Jewish faith). These seven were presented to the apostles, who prayed for them as they laid their hands on them.

We could argue that running a food program was perceived by the twelve apostles as an individual-level form of leadership like the example of the nonprofit leader whose focus is just on providing resources for an afterschool program. The twelve apostles knew that if they were going to build the church, they couldn't be focused on an individual level of advocacy. Yes, they needed to fix discriminating practices imposed by Hebrew-speaking believers, but that couldn't be their only focus. Instead, they knew they had to focus on systemic and broader levels of advocacy by spending time teaching the word of God and in prayer. Their solution? Hire other leaders to focus on individual-level advocacy while they focused on systemic and broader levels of advocacy. That is where leaders today need to operate.

Let's look at the second example of the three levels of advocacy with a story of Moses in Exodus 18:14–23 (NLT).

> When Moses' father-in-law saw all that Moses was doing for the people, he asked, "What are you really accomplishing here? Why are you trying to do all this alone while everyone stands around you from morning till evening?" Moses replied, "Because the people come to me to get a ruling from God. When a dispute arises, they come to me, and I am the one who settles the case

between the quarreling parties. I inform the people of God's decrees and give them his instructions."

"This is not good!" Moses' father-in-law exclaimed. "You're going to wear yourself out—and the people, too. This job is too heavy a burden for you to handle all by yourself. Now listen to me, and let me give you a word of advice, and may God be with you. You should continue to be the people's representative before God, bringing their disputes to him. Teach them God's decrees, and give them his instructions. Show them how to conduct their lives. But select from all the people some capable, honest men who fear God and hate bribes. Appoint them as leaders over groups of one thousand, one hundred, fifty, and ten. They should always be available to solve the people's common disputes, but have them bring the major cases to you. Let the leaders decide the smaller matters themselves. They will help you carry the load, making the task easier for you. If you follow this advice, and if God commands you to do so, then you will be able to endure the pressures, and all these people will go home in peace."

We see here that Moses is a leader on the path of exhaustion and burnout. Why? Because he's a systemic and broader leader functioning on an individual level. Day and night, and night and day, the people of Israel stood before Moses for him to settle cases of indifference. Can you imagine the sort of issues they were bringing before him? "Someone stole my goat and I want it back" or perhaps "My neighbor's boundary line crosses over into my property line and we need to reestablish our property lines." Moses was operating on an individual level of advocacy. His father-in-law saw this and recommended that he hire leaders to settle small and common disputes (individual level) while Moses worked on major cases, teaching the people God's decrees and instructions, and representing the people before God (systemic and broader advocacy).

There are two vital points. First, the twelve apostles and Moses would be considered high-level leaders (that is, pastors, senior leadership, executive directors, CEOs, and so forth) in today's context. Their focus was on prayer, administering biblical truths to the people, and leading from a systemic and broader advocacy approach. In both cases, God had both the twelve apostles and Moses operating on a systemic and broader level of advocacy.

Imagine for a moment, if God told Moses to concentrate his time and energy on settling small, common disputes for the rest of his life, or he told the twelve apostles to focus on running the food program. Again, both are needed services, but who would be the leader moving initiatives? Where would the children of Israel have gone if Moses hadn't led? What would have happened to the early church if the twelve apostles had been running food programs? The role of high-level Christian leaders is to advocate on systemic and broader levels to transform systems, institutions, and culture to produce kingdom-minded followers of Christ across diverse people groups.

The second vital point is the hiring of leaders who can operate at the individual level. Not everyone is called to a high-level leadership position, but individual-level leaders are of extreme importance to the systemic- and broader-level leader. For Moses to effectively produce results from his high-level position, he needed trustworthy and high-functioning leaders to oversee the individual level of settling small, common disputes. For the twelve apostles to effectively pioneer the early church, they needed individual-level leaders overseeing the food program.

This is the idea of the diversity of roles within the body of Christ (see Romans 12:4–5). Leaders on different levels are needed to accomplish the bigger vision of the organization. When advocating on behalf of marginalized people or communities, high-level leaders must move beyond "food programs" and "small and common disputes" to facilitate change within systemic and broader levels of organizations and society.

Joint Agenda

An important piece often left out in the Advocacy stage is where both groups can sit down together and develop programming, services, opportunities, and so forth. In the education sector, many researchers have found that the outcomes of joint agenda-sharing are highly beneficial. Research conducted by Marsh (2007) on community-district partnerships showed that collaboration with joint participation enacted a democratic intent and was able to implement a successful joint action plan.

We are putting into motion the three previous stages (Understand, Learn, Relate) we have gone through. This is your opportunity to shine! Engagement and advocacy give voice to the people of the marginalized and facilitate their participation in achieving their objectives and goals (Lasker and Weiss, 2003). I want to share a powerful quote from one of my interviews with a leader of a Christian organization. When discussing the importance of collaboration with marginalized people groups regarding programming, the leader said, "I think also making sure that what it is that your organization [does]—whatever their mission is, whatever their goal is—aligns with the community as well, because if you have maybe some sort of programming that you're offering, [but] the community's not in need of that, then that's not beneficial to anybody."

Too many organizations have come into marginalized communities and have established programming and services without a strong process to collaborate with the actual people they are seeking to serve. Although most organizations have the best intentions, quickly implementing what they think is best for the community, which gets them labeled as "saviors," trust takes a much longer time to develop, if at all. Sensoy and Ali-Khan (2016) and Gorski (2008) recognized that having the best intentions is insufficient and only perpetuates hierarchical norms. Straubhaar (2015) defines savior as "The idea that socially privileged individuals possess, simply by virtue of their position, some unique ability or power to help less-privileged people in ways they're unable to help themselves."

Interestingly enough, during my research the phrase *white savior* or *savior* was a common theme stated by marginalized people over and over again. When I discussed these terms with Christian leaders of nonprofits and churches, another common theme emerged among them. It was the idea that by highlighting the deficiencies of marginalized people groups and communities, they can excite funders/donors to give resources to solve that particular deficit, thus creating a story of saving where the funder/donor is the hero. Although this wasn't a theme I expected in the research, I couldn't ignore the findings.

After continuing to develop this idea of savior, I interviewed funders/donors and found that many of them did indeed see themselves as saving others. "We gave them a playground; I don't understand why they don't use it" is a quote by one donor. Another donor, when asked why he gives, stated, "Because the parents don't care about their kids, so I give [in order] to give them an opportunity to have food and homework help after school." The mindset of the savior complex is the antithesis of advocacy work and everything the model stands for. Yet, I have found it to be an ongoing ideology within leadership teams when working across cultures.

It's a deficit-thinking approach to engagement, which hinders relationship-building efforts. Think about it: when you are building a friendship with someone, are you focused on their deficits or bad habits, or are you intrigued with what they can bring to the table in a friendship? You're attracted to something about them, whether it's their personality or a spiritual gift. Or they're a sports fan just like you! The same thing applies when building relationships and advocacy work across diverse cultures. The focus isn't on what they lack; it's on what they can bring to the table, especially if it's unique to you. The reason why leaders don't recognize it in different cultures is that they don't know what to look for *and* they are looking for what is common to them.

Here are some points to consider when thinking through joint agenda sharing.

- Involve those who are being served early in the process, not later.
- Consider the cultural practices and understandings of the people being served.
- Think of transforming systemic levels, not individual levels, but engage on individual levels, not systemic levels.
- Your norms might not be their norms; be attentive.
- Think democracy, not dictatorship.

Advocacy work is tough work. God has called leaders to systemic and broader levels of advocacy, and engaging cross-culturally takes work. It takes effort, but the rewards of engaging collaboratively are priceless. Setting up systems where every voice is heard and everyone gets a seat at the decision-making table is crucial. Cornell West (2005) stated the following.

> All systems set up to enact democracy are subject to corrupt manipulations, and that is why the public commitment to democratic involvement is so vital. Genuine, robust democracy must be brought to life through democratic individuality, democratic community, and democratic society (p. 103).

In Philippians 2:1–3, Paul called us to advocacy.

> Therefore if you have any encouragement from being united with Christ, if any comfort from his love, if any common sharing in the Spirit, if any tenderness and compassion, then make my joy complete by being like-minded, having the same love, being one in spirit and of one mind. Do nothing out of selfish ambition or vain conceit. Rather, in humility value others above yourselves.

Only with this mindset can we perform the true advocacy that moves mountains.

STAGE 5: PARTICIPATE THROUGH UNITY

Stage 5 of the cross-cultural model of collaboration is participation. Based on the joint goals developed in the Advocacy stage, everyone has a role to play regarding specific programming and services that can be put into action. Participation is twofold. One, we have more involvement from marginalized people or the community because they were involved in planning the program or service. Two, all programs and services need a measurement and assessment component. But how do you measure cultural competence and collaboration? From a biblical perspective, there are three key indicators that cross-cultural collaboration is on the right track: unity, producing, and growth.

Unity, Not Diversity

Unity is a word that is central to the Christian faith. The Bible is clear, specifically in Jesus's ministry, that unity is what God is looking for. Listen to Jesus's prayer to God on behalf of all followers of him in John 17:20–26 (NIV).

> My prayer is not for them alone. I pray also for those who will believe in me through their message, that all of them may be one, Father, just as you are in me and I am in you. May they also be in us so that the world may believe that you have sent me. I have given them the glory that you gave me, that they may be one as we are one—I in them and you in me—so that they may be brought to complete unity. Then the world will know that you sent me and have loved them even as you have loved me. Father, I want those you have given me to be with me where I am, and to see my glory, the glory you have given me because you loved me before the creation of the world. Righteous Father, though the world does not know you, I know you, and they know that you

have sent me. I have made you known to them and will
continue to make you known in order that the love you
have for me may be in them and that I myself may be
in them.

This is a powerful prayer on unity, but pay particular attention to verses twenty-two and twenty-three: "I have given them the glory that you gave me, that they may be one as we are one—I in them and you in me—so that they may be brought to complete unity. Then the world will know that you sent me and have loved them even as you have loved me." Jesus's prayer is for all believers to become one as "we" [Jesus and God] are one. Why? Because being one is being brought into complete unity. For what purpose? "Then the world will know that you sent me and have loved them."

To break this down further, let's look at a few concepts. First, unity doesn't mean diversity. Yet, too many of our Christian organizations operate as if these terms have equal meaning. Diversity simply means a variety or an array of things that are different. For example, you can have five apples in front of you. Diversity could be measured by color (green, red, and yellow), taste (bitter or sweet), size (large to small), and so forth.

Unity on the other hand is a little more complex to measure. When you think of a wedding, the scripture most often quoted is Genesis 2:24 (NASB), "For this reason a man shall leave his father and his mother, and be joined to his wife; and they shall become one flesh." Unity is becoming one flesh, not different flesh (diversity). Think about an artist. When artists paint a portrait, they are using diverse colors, patterns, shapes, depth, size, etc., to form a painting that is united. Two different (diverse) individuals get married and become one (united). All the different elements (diversity) combine to go into a beautiful piece of painting (united). What Jesus is referring to is that he and God are two different beings but are united as one. His prayer is that his followers will do the same. Simply put, unity is diversity married.

When diversity started becoming a hot topic for HR leaders in the corporate world many decades ago because of changes in the law (the US Equal Employment Opportunity Act, for example), it was easy to measure. Look at the organization that you lead: you can easily measure and assess diversity using a quantitative analysis. Quantitative analysis consists of something that can be counted, measured, and expressed using numbers. You can count the number of participants based on the category they associate with—that is, gender, race, age, and so forth.

Something I do with each client, where applicable, is go to their website, click on the "About Me" or "Who We Are" section, and see whether diversity exists. I can quickly assess the leadership team and the staff visually using quantitative analysis. For example, if I see a leadership team that is homogenous—that is, twelve white men or twelve youth—I can quickly deduce potential challenges within the team from a quantitative perspective. On the contrary, if I view a team of twelve who is diverse visually—that is, gender, race, age, and so forth—I can easily fall into the trap and say it's a united team.

However, remember you can't assess unity using the same quantitative measures. Unity has to be measured using qualitative measures, which analyze data based on behaviors, characteristics, and traits. The way this is measured is through one-on-one interviews, focus groups, surveys, feedback forms, exit interviews, and so forth. The unity that Jesus is referring to is a true, authentic relationship that can be measured by how one **feels** toward the other. God felt love for his son, Jesus, as expressed in Matthew 3:17 (NIV), "This is my Son, whom I love." Jesus felt love for his father, God, found in John 14:31 (NIV), "but he [Jesus] comes so that the world may learn that I love the Father and do exactly what my Father has commanded me." Unity can be measured by love. Consider reflecting on these questions.

How much biblically based love do I have for a person who is culturally the same and culturally different from me? Is my love the same despite cultural differences? Is my love only for those who look, think, act, and behave like me? Do I love at all?

A second concept is that there is a purpose for unity. Unity isn't just a feel-good thing or a superficial alliance of diverse people. Jesus clearly states in John 17:23 (NIV), "Then the world will know that you sent me and have loved them even as you have loved me." This is how the witness of the church is to be made to a lost world. When the lost world sees unity within followers of Christ, the world understands that Jesus came for them, died for them, rose again for them, and is coming back for them. They begin to understand God's love for them, his grace, and his mercy.

Unfortunately, the world is not seeing a unified body of Christ. In 1963, Dr. Martin Luther King Jr. said, "It is appalling that the most segregated hour of Christian America is eleven o'clock on Sunday morning." A strong argument can be had that things haven't changed much since then. The church is still, in my opinion, not unified, using the framework of love that Jesus talked about in John 17. Have things improved since this quote in 1963? It really depends on whom you ask. Based on my experiences and the years of consulting work I have done with Christian organizations, I would argue that they remain the same but are disguised differently. There is a superficial unity that is taking place. Basically, Christian organizations are selling unity as a qualitative story, when in actuality, it's merely a quantitative feature.

I have talked to hundreds, if not thousands, of Christian leaders, other Christians, non-Christians, parishioners, staff, community leaders, and more over the years. I have heard stories of great unity, and I have heard stories of great disunity. Recently, I met with a black worship leader who recently left a majority white megachurch. She shared with me the racism, microaggressions, stereotypes, and discrimination she faced from parishioners and colleagues *in the church*. She was told things like, "You are too dark-skinned to wear dark clothes; we can't see you" and "Sing our type of music, not black music." When she approached church leaders, they basically told her that there was nothing they could do about it. Unity across cultures was an issue for the early church back in the days of the twelve apostles, and over 2,000 years later, we are still dealing with the same issues.

Producing: Making Things Happen

Producing is important in the life of the followers of Christ. Many, including me, believe that every individual was put on this earth for a purpose, and that purpose leads us to produce an outcome. One of my biggest pet peeves is a lazy person. Every individual has been given gifts, talents, dreams, abilities, skills, and purpose to positively contribute to society. It's the same with organizations. If your organization is not producing results because of a lack of unity, then you are wasting valuable resources and, more important, time. Now, I'm not saying that unity guarantees success, but I would argue that unity drastically increases the chances of success and participation.

Let me give you an example using our nonprofit leader and the afterschool program. If a nonprofit group decides to open an afterschool program in a historically marginalized community and does not seek a true, authentic collaboration with the people in that community, the chances of impact and participation drastically decrease.

Yes, the group will have a couple of success stories that will keep it afloat and make the funders happy for a while, but to have a kingdom-minded impact, the group needs to operate on those higher levels of advocacy: systemic and broader. Through unity, producing occurs, which yields results.

Let's examine two passages of scripture to illustrate results.

- Psalm 1:3 (ESV): "He is like a tree planted by streams of water that yields its fruit in its season, and its leaf does not wither. In all that he does, he prospers."
- Galatians 5:22–23 (NIV): "But the fruit of the Spirit is love, joy, peace, patience, kindness, goodness, faithfulness, gentleness and self-control."

In these passages, we see two types of results for *fruit*. The one in the Psalm refer to *fruit* as works, actions, and deeds. Think of this kind of fruit as the fruit you can see, smell, feel, and taste. It's something you can quantify or perhaps describe the quality of. The *fruit* in Galatians describes the qualities, gifts, or attributes of something. Therefore, we could say that through the *fruit* of the spirit (love, joy, peace, patience, kindness, goodness, faithfulness, gentleness, and self-control), a follower of Christ can yield *fruit* in season. These results come from a life that is representative of Christian character through the Holy Spirit. In other words, *fruit* (Galatians 5:22–23) is not something we can produce through self-efficacy; it's only through the work of the Holy Spirit in our lives. We are obligated to live a life by the Spirit (Galatians 5:16) to yield the *fruit* found in Psalm 1:3.

If we are to produce unity within cross-cultural collaboration, we must produce the character of a Christ follower through understanding and loving others from a biblical perspective. From there, we produce tangible fruit (works, deeds, and actions) that contribute to the participation stage of the model. Look at this verse to understand how both *fruits* work in unison: Matthew 7:17–20 (NIV).

> Likewise, every good tree bears good fruit, but a bad tree bears bad fruit. A good tree cannot bear bad fruit, and a bad tree cannot bear good fruit. Every tree that does not bear good fruit is cut down and thrown into the fire. Thus, by their fruit you will recognize them.

Pay particular attention to verse 18, "a good tree." The Galatians 5:22–23 fruit cannot bear bad fruit (Psalm 1:3). The good tree represents the character of a Christ follower; the bearing fruit is the outcome that flows from the character. There is a direct biblical correlation between producing and growth.

Growth

When the church was being formed in the book of Acts, we get a glimpse in the following scriptures (emphasis added) of the transformative way the church today might grow.

- Acts 2:41–42 (NIV): "Those who accepted his message were baptized, and about three thousand were *added* to their number that day. **They devoted themselves to the apostles' teaching and to the fellowship**, to the breaking of bread and to prayer."
- Acts 4:31–33 (NIV): "After they prayed, the place where they were meeting was shaken. And they were all filled with the Holy Spirit and spoke the word of God boldly. **All the**

believers were one in heart in mind. No one claimed that any of his possessions was his own, but they shared everything they had. With great power the apostles continued to testify to the resurrection of the Lord Jesus, and *much grace was upon them all.*"

- Acts 5:12, 14 (NIV): "The apostles performed many signs and wonders among the people. **And all the believers used to meet together** in Solomon's Colonnade ... *more and more men and women* believed in the Lord and were *added* to their number."

In the beginning of Acts 6, we saw advocacy work being conducted because of discriminatory practices. As the twelve apostles worked out a solution to bring unity among the believers, we now see the result of the unity later in the chapter.

- Acts 6:5, 7 (NIV): "The proposal **pleased the whole group** ... So the word of God spread. *The number of disciples in Jerusalem increased rapidly,* and a large number of priests become obedient to the faith."

The theme here is that where there is unity in Christ, there is growth. The church went from *adding* numbers to *multiplying* numbers because they were united. It's that simple! Growth doesn't just happen because you have a strong vision or mission statement. It doesn't just happen if you are fiscally sound. It doesn't just happen because you are well liked. Biblically speaking, growth comes through unity, and unity comes from being one with each other and with God.

Growth also comes to the individual. Colossians 1:10 (NIV) tells us, "So that you may live a life worthy of the Lord and please him in every way: bearing fruit in every good work, growing in the knowledge of God." As believers in Christ, we are commanded to grow in the faith. One of my favorite verses in the Bible is John 8:31–32 (NIV), where Jesus says, "To the Jews who had believed him, Jesus said, 'If you hold to my teaching, you are really my disciples. Then you will know the truth, and the truth will set you free.'"

I believe there is direct correlation between being set free from the truth and transformation. Once we know or are exposed to the truth, the truth should transform us. For example, once there is an awareness of systemic racism that exists in the church and in society, that truth should transform us to rebuke and denounce it because its clear message is contrary to the Word of God. We should always be growing, both individually and collectively. That is biblical truth.

CONCLUSION

The cross-cultural model of collaboration illustrates the five-point cyclical process in cross-cultural collaborative and relationship efforts. The model is meant to be sequential but does not have to be. For example, if our nonprofit leader was introduced to a historically marginalized community in the Participate stage—that is, a neighborhood cleanup endeavor or a movies-in-the-park event—the leader should participate but would eventually go through the steps in the model to build true, authentic collaboration and relationships if he or she seeks opportunities to serve that community.

Another example would be if our nonprofit leader already had a relationship with a culturally different community leader or group, he or she could come into the community but still would need to work through the stages of the model in order to have a true collaborative experience. As a reminder, this model is not a one-time-and-done model. It's a lifelong journey of learning and, more important, becoming more Christ-like when engaging others from diverse cultures.

Early European immigrants came to the New World with the mission to expand Christianity. They were passionately and deeply motivated to "make Christians" out of everyone. Today, followers of Christ still feel the call to spread the gospel message to all who will hear and receive the call of repentance and salvation. While this is the essence of the Great Commission (Matthew 28:18–20), that's not all there is to it. Once a person becomes a follower of Christ, there is work to be done. We all are on our personal journey to become more Christ-like such that we begin understanding and displaying the fruits of the spirit in our lives.

The way you love and ultimately treat others is a direct indication of what "fruit" you have growing in your heart. In Micah 6:8 (NIV), we read, "He has shown you, O mortal, what is good. And what does the Lord require of you? To act justly and to love mercy and to walk humbly with your God." To act justly means to treat others the way you would like to be treated—that is, in a fair and just manner. Next, God says *love* mercy rather than just *show* mercy. Jesus says in Matthew 7:1 (NIV), "Do not judge, or you too will be judged." The same love for mercy we expect from God is the same love for mercy we need to show others. The call for all believers is to seek justice by fighting injustices. The Bible is full of scriptures telling followers of Christ to fight injustices. Here are a few for your consideration.

- Isaiah 1:17—Learn to do good; seek justice, reprove the ruthless, defend the orphan, plead for the widow.
- Hosea 10:13—You have plowed wickedness, you have repeated injustice, you have eaten the fruit of lies.

- Romans 1:18—For the wrath of God is revealed from heaven against all ungodliness and unrighteousness of men who suppress the truth in unrighteousness.
- Proverbs 21:3—To do righteousness and justice is desired by the Lord more than sacrifice.

Simply put, God hates injustice and commands us to fight against it. This is not only an individual mandate, but a body-of-Christ mandate. Proverbs 21:3 and Micah 6:8 capture the essential work that all followers of Christ should be undertaking. Unfortunately, many Christian leaders have turned a blind eye toward justice work in the name of maintaining a neutral stance within their organizations, being careful to not disrupt our Christian cultural norms. It pains me to see the capacity of organizations to make a huge difference but choose not to in order to maintain norms.

I have many, many stories and examples of Christians sitting on the fence, including myself for some time, when it comes to fighting injustices within our communities and our country. Jesus gave a stark warning to those of us who are on the fence in Revelation 3:15–17 (NIV).

> I know your deeds, that you are neither cold nor hot. I wish you were either one or the other! So, because you are lukewarm—neither hot nor cold—I am about to spit you out of my mouth. You say, "I am rich; I have acquired wealth and do not need a thing." But you do not realize that you are wretched, pitiful, poor, blind and naked.

I believe every Christian leader should ask themselves this question: "Do I have the capacity to do more on a higher level?" I reflect on this every day. As a leader and trainer of leaders, I want to make a huge impact on the kingdom of God, but I also want to be a part of a larger change initiative, where systems are disrupted in the name of justice. I personally believe that is the level where God wants many leaders to operate. It might not be within their own organizations, but being a part of a larger, systemic movement is where Christian leaders have the opportunity to invite God into that space. For example, a Christian leader might volunteer his or her time to engage in a community project that seeks to provide economic opportunities and better access to marginalized people groups or to volunteer time at his or her church to provide input into programs or services that break down barriers for immigrants in their communities.

The body of Christ needs leaders who have a justice mindset. Justice seeks to provide fair ground for everyone, and leaders have tremendous opportunities to provide impactful processes and endeavors. My challenge to all Christian leaders is to look within yourselves and the organizations you lead with a justice framework and simply ask the question, Can we be doing something better or can we be doing more? I truly believe we can. Adrian Pei (2018) put it eloquently when he simply said the following.

- Leaders who are in touch with *pain* can see and serve people with *compassion*.
- Leaders who are in touch with *power* can become incredible *advocates* for the most vulnerable in society.
- Leaders who are in touch with the *past* can teach and guide others with great *humility* and *wisdom*.

This book gives you a basic understanding of what we need to do to move forward with cross-cultural collaboration within the context of the Christian church in the United States. I suggest using the book as a tool to learn cross-cultural interactions and collaboration. My hope and prayer is that you yield yourself to the work of the Holy Spirit. In 1 Thessalonians 5:21, Paul said to test things and hold on to what is good. I don't proclaim, nor will I ever, to have a 100 percent understanding of cross-cultural interactions. We are all learning and growing together to become more Christ-like. I am truly happy to share my research and thoughts in this book, and I pray that God will speak to you.

I want to leave you with this thought.

Acts 2:42–47 presents a beautiful picture of a cross-cultural community. After Peter preached a moving sermon, about three thousand people came to Christ that day. Diverse groups of people from all over the region were present during this sermon (v. 9–11). The new believers immediately had a commonality (v. 44): they all believed in Jesus Christ, were baptized with the Holy Spirit, and began living as a community. They tended to the needs of one another, shared meals together, devoted themselves to listening and growing by the teachings of the apostles, and, just as important, lived life together. They had one common goal and rallied around that goal as a community.

Cultural differences do not matter when we rally behind one goal. Race does not matter when we rally behind one goal. There is one race, the human race.

REFERENCES

Abdullah, H. (2020). "What Do Terms Like Systemic Racism, Microaggression and White Fragility Mean?" *ABC News*. https://abcnews.go.com/Politics/terms-systemic-racism-microaggression-white-fragility/story?id=71195820.

Adams, J.T. (1931). *The Epic of America*. Boston: Little, Brown.

"Ally" in *Merriam-Webster Dictionary* (11th ed.). Springfield, Massachusetts: Merriam-Webster.

"Allyship" in *Merriam-Webster Dictionary* (11th ed.). Springfield, Massachusetts: Merriam-Webster.

Anderson, G. (2009). *Advocacy Leadership: Toward a Post-Reform Agenda in Education*. New York: Routledge.

Angelo, Maya. "How to Write—and How to Live" From the April 2011 issue of *O, The Oprah Magazine* http://www.oprah.com/spirit/how-to-write-a-poem-maya-angelous-advice/all#ixzz6Zk5YMWby.

Argyris, C., and Schon, D. (1974). *Theory in Practice: Increasing Professional Effectiveness*. San Francisco: Jossey Bass.

Argyris, C. (1999). *On Organizational Learning*. Cambridge: Blackwell.

Atcheson, S. (2018). "Allyship—The Key to Unlocking the Power of Diversity." https://www.forbes.com/sites/shereeatcheson/2018/11/30/allyship-the-key-to-unlocking-the-power-of-diversity/#5ff477649c6f.

Avruch, K. (1998). *Culture and Conflict Resolution*. Washington, DC: United States Institute of Peace Press.

Ayman, R., and Korabik, K. (2010). "Leadership: Why Gender and Culture Matter." *American Psychologist* 65 (3). 157.

Baker, K.G., and Gippenreiter, J.B. (1998). "Stalin's Purge and Its Impact on Russian Families." In Danieli, Y. (ed.). *International Handbook of Multigenerational Legacies of Trauma*. New York: Plenum Press. 403–434.

Bamberg, M. (2004). "Considering Counter-Narratives." In Bamberg, M., and Andrews, M. (eds.). *Considering Counter-Narratives: Narrating, Resisting, Making Sense*. Amsterdam, The Netherlands: John Benjamins. 351–371.

Bamberg, M., and Andrews, M. (eds.). (2004). *Considering Counter-Narratives. Narrating, Resisting, Making Sense*. Amsterdam, The Netherlands: John Benjamins.

Beachum, F.D., Dentith, A.M., McCray, C.R., and Boyle, T. (2008). "Havens of Hope or the Killing Fields: The Paradox of Leadership, Pedagogy, and Relationships in an Urban Middle School." *Urban Education* 43. 189–215. doi: 10.1177/0042085907312329.

Beresford, C. (1900). "The Future of the Anglo-Saxon Race." *The North American Review* 171 (529). 802–810.

Bolin, B., Grineski, S., and Collins, T. (2005). "The Geography of Despair: Environmental Racism and the Making of South Phoenix, Arizona, USA." *Human Ecology Review* 12 (2). 156.

Bomer, R., Dworin, J.E., May, L., and Semingson, P. (2008). "Miseducating Teachers about the Poor: A Critical Analysis

of Ruby Payne's Claims about Poverty." *Teachers College Record* 110 (12). 2497–2531.
Bonilla-Silva, E. (2006). *Racism without Racists: Color-Blind Racism and the Persistence of Racial Inequality in the United States*. Lanham: Rowman & Littlefield.
Bourdieu, P., and Passeron, J.C. (1977). *Reproduction in Education, Society and Culture*. London: Sage Publications.
Bourdieu, P. (1986). "The Forms of Capital." In Richardson, J.G. (ed.). *Handbook of Theory and Research for the Sociology of Education*. New York: Greenwood Press. 241–258.
Brave Heart, M.Y., and DeBruyn, L.M. (1998). "The American Indian Holocaust: Healing Historical Unresolved Grief." *American Indian and Alaska Native Mental Health Research* 8 (2). 56–78.
Brayboy, B.M.J., Castagno, A.E., and Maughan, E. (2007). "Equality and Justice for All? Examining Race in Education Scholarship." *Review of Research in Education* 31. 159–194. doi: 10.3102/0091732X07300045.
Brown, B. (2013). "The Power of Empathy." Animation by Katy Davis. https://www.thersa.org/discover/videos/rsa-shorts/2013/12/Brene-Brown-on-Empathy.
Campbell, C.D., Evans-Campbell, T. (2011). "Historical Trauma and Native American Child Development and Mental Health: An Overview." In Sarche, M., Spicer, P., Farrell, P., and Fitzgerald, H.E. (eds.). *American Indian and Alaska Native Children and Mental Health: Development, Context, Prevention, and Treatment*. Santa Barbara, California: Praeger. 1–26.
Cann, C.N., and McCloskey, E. (2017). "The Poverty Pimpin' Project: How Whiteness Profits from Black and Brown Bodies in Community Service Programs." *Race Ethnicity and Education* 20 (1). 72–86.

Cartwright, S. (2002). "Double-Loop Learning: A Concept and Process for Leadership Educators." *Journal of Leadership Education* 1 (1). 68–71.

Cherry, K. (2020). "How Does Implicit Bias Influence Behavior?" *Explanations and Impacts of Unconscious Bias.* https://www.verywellmind.com/implicit-bias-overview-4178401

Chubbuck, S.M. (2004). "Whiteness Enacted, Whiteness Disrupted: The Complexity of Personal Congruence." *American Educational Research Journal* 41 (2). 301–333.

Collins, L., and Barnes, S.L. (2014). "Observing Privilege: Examining Race, Class, and Gender in Health and Human Service Organizations." *Journal for Social Action in Counseling and Psychology* 6 (1). 61.

Connell, R.W. (1998). "RW Connell's 'Masculinities': Reply." *Gender and Society* 12 (4). 474–477.

Daud, A., Skoglund, E., and Rydelius, P.A. (2005). "Children in Families of Torture Victims: Transgenerational Transmission of Parents' Traumatic Experiences to Their Children." *International Journal of Social Welfare* 14 (1). 23–32.

Davis, B.W., Gooden, M.A., and Micheaux, D.J. (2015). "Color-Blind Leadership: A Critical Race Theory Analysis of the ISLLC and ELCC Standards." *Educational Administration Quarterly* 51 (3). 335–371. doi: 10.1177/0013161X15587092.

Dein, S. (2006). "Race, Culture and Ethnicity in Minority Research: A Critical Discussion." *Journal of Cultural Diversity* 13 (2). 68. Adapted from a Living in Harmony Funded Project, "Culture and Colour," Northern Beaches Neighbourhood Service, New South Wales, 2005.

Feagin, J.R. (2004). "Toward an Integrated Theory of Systemic Racism." *The Changing Terrain of Race and Ethnicity.* 203–223.

Feagin, J. (2013). *Systemic Racism: A Theory of Oppression*. New York: Routledge.

"Federal Acts and Assimilation Policies." Minnesota Historical Society. https://www.usdakotawar.org/history/newcomers-us-government-and-military/acts-policy.

Frye, M. (1983). "On Being White: Thinking toward a Feminist Understanding of Race and Race Supremacy." In Burg, T. (ed.). *Politics of Reality: Essays in Feminist Theory*. New York: Crossing Press.

Future of the Two Races. What the South Owes the Negro, and What His Place in Progress Should Be—The Wonderful Possibilities of the South. Address of Hon. Henry W. Grady, of Atlanta, Georgia, Delivered at Dallas, Texas, October 27, 1888.

Goetz, R.A. (2016). *The Baptism of Early Virginia: How Christianity Created Race*. Baltimore: Johns Hopkins University Press.

Gordon, J. (2010). *Soup: A Recipe to Nourish Your Team and Culture*. Hoboken, NJ: Wiley.

Gorski, P. (2008). "Good Intentions Are Not Enough: A Decolonizing Intercultural Education." *Intercultural Education* 19 (6). 515–525.

Haynes, S.R. (2007). *Noah's Curse: The Biblical Justification of American Slavery*. Oxford: Oxford University Press.

Henry, F., and Tator, C. (2006). *The Colour of Democracy: Racism in Canadian Society* (3rd ed.). Toronto: Nelson.

History.com Editors. (2019). "Manifest Destiny." https://www.history.com/topics/westward-expansion/manifest-destiny.

Hochschild, J.L. (1995). *Facing Up to the American Dream: Race, Class, and the Soul of the Nation*. Princeton, New Jersey: Princeton University Press.

Johnson, A.G. (2006). *Privilege, Power, and Difference* (2nd ed.). Boston: McGraw-Hill.

Karenian, H., Livaditis, M., Karenian, S., Zafiriadis, K., Bochtsou, V., and Xenitidis, K. (2011). "Collective Trauma Transmission and Traumatic Reactions among Descendants of Armenian Refugees." *International Journal of Social Psychiatry* 57 (4). 327–337.

Kellermann, N.P. (2001). "Psychopathology in Children of Holocaust Survivors: A Review of The Research Literature." *Israeli Journal of Psychiatry Related Science* 38 (1). 36–46.

Kendall, F.E. (2001). *Understanding White Privilege*. Albany, CA: California Alumni Association.

Khalifa, M., Arnold, N. W., & Newcomb, W. (2015). Understand and advocate for communities first. *Phi Delta Kappan*, 96 (7). 20–25.

Kivel, P. (1996). *Uprooting Racism: How White People Can Work for Racial Justice*. Gabriola Island, British Columbia, Canada: New Society Press.

Kolb, K.H. (2007). "Supporting Our Black Men: Reproducing Male Privilege in a Black Student Political Organization." *Sociological Spectrum* 27 (3). 257–274.

Kroeber, A.L., & Kluckhohn, C. (1952). Culture: a critical review of concepts and definitions. *Papers. Peabody Museum of Archaeology & Ethnology, Harvard University*, 47 (1). viii, 223.

Ladson-Billings, G. (1996). "Silence as Weapons: Challenges of Black Professor Teaching White Students." *Theory into Practice* 35 (2). 79–85.

Lasker, R.D., and Weiss, E.S. (2003). "Broadening Participation in Community Problem Solving: A Multidisciplinary Model to Support Collaborative Practice and Research." *Journal of Urban Health* 80 (1). 14–47.

Lebrón, A. (2013). "What Is Culture?" *Merit Research Journal of Education and Review* 1 (6). 126–132.

LeChasseur, K. (2014). "Critical Race Theory and the Meaning of 'Community' in District Partnerships." *Equity and Excellence in Education* 47 (3). 305–320.

Leonardo, Zeus. (2004). "The color of supremacy: Beyond the discourse of 'white privilege'." *Educational Philosophy and Theory* 36 (2). 137–152.

Lewis, A. (2004). "'What Group?' Studying Whites and Whiteness in the Era of 'Color-Blindness.'" *Sociological Theory* 22 (4). 623–646.

Liou, D.D., Antrop-González, R., and Cooper, R. (2009). "Unveiling the Promise of Community Cultural Wealth to Sustaining Latina/o Students' College-Going Information Networks." *Educational Studies* 45. 534–555.

Lipsitz, G. (n.d.). *The Possessive Investment in Whiteness: How White People Profit from Identity Politics.* Philadelphia, PA: Temple University Press.

Loewen, J.W. (2007). *Lies My Teacher Told Me: Everything Your American History Textbook Got Wrong.* New York: Simon & Schuster.

Lowe, F. (2013). "Keeping Leadership White: Invisible Blocks to Black Leadership and Its Denial in White Organizations." *Journal of Social Work Practice* 27 (2). 149–162.

Martínez, E. (2016). "What Is White Supremacy?" *SOA Watch: Close the School of the Americas.* https://www.nosue.org/app/download/7244496066/what-is-white-supremacy.pdf.

Marsh, J. A. (2007). *Democratic dilemmas: Joint work, education politics, and community.* Albany, NY: SUNY Press.

Mason, E. (2018). *Woke Church: An Urgent Call for Christians in America to Confront Racism and Injustice.* Chicago, IL: Moody.

Matsumoto, D. (1996). *Culture and Psychology.* Pacific Grove, California: Brooks/Cole.

Mawn, G.P. (1979). "Phoenix: Arizona: Central City of the Southwest, 1870–1920. Volumes 1–2." Doctoral dissertation. Arizona State University, Tempe, Arizona.

McIntosh, P. (1988). *White Privilege: Unpacking the Invisible Knapsack.* Peggy McIntosh is associate director of the Wellesley Collage Center for Research on Women. This essay is excerpted from Working Paper 189. "White Privilege and Male Privilege: A Personal Account of Coming To See Correspondences through Work in Women's Studies" (1988), by Peggy McIntosh; available for $4.00 from the Wellesley College Center for Research on Women, Wellesley MA 02181 The working paper contains a longer list of privileges. This excerpted essay is reprinted from the Winter 1990 issue of Independent school.

McLucas, A.C. (2003). *Decision Making: Risk Management, Systems Thinking and Situation Awareness.* Canberra: Argos Press.

"Meritocracy" in *Merriam-Webster Dictionary* (11th ed.). Springfield, Massachusetts: Merriam-Webster.

Meshchaninov, Y. (2012). "The Prussian-Industrial History of Public Schooling." *The New American Academy.* http://www.dontcomply.com/wp-content/uploads/2015/09/the-prussian-industrial-history-of-public-schooling1.pdf

Mintzberg, H. (1994). *The Rise and Fall of Strategic Planning: Reconceiving Roles for Planning, Plans, and Planners.* New York: The Free Press. 368.

Mohatt, N.V., Thompson, A.B., Thai, N.D., and Tebes, J.K. (2014). "Historical Trauma as Public Narrative: A Conceptual Review of How History Impacts Present-Day Health." *Social Science and Medicine* 106. 128–136.

Montero, M. (2009). "Methods for Liberation: Critical Consciousness in Action." In Montero, M., and Sonn, C.C. (eds.). *Psychology and Liberation: Theory and Applications.* New York: Springer. 73–91.

Nademin, E. (2019). *Don't Be a Stranger* (1st ed.). Scottsdale, Arizona: Elicia Nademin, Ph.D., LLC.

Neblett, B.J. (2009). "George." http://bjneblett.blogspot.com/2013/02/george-part-one.html.

Nelson, R.K. Winling, L., Marciano, R., Connolly, N., et al. "Mapping Inequality." in Nelson, R.K., and Ayers, E.L. (eds.). *American Panorama.* https://dsl.richmond.edu/panorama/redlining/#loc=5/37.8/-97.9&text=downloads.

Noblit, G.W. (2015). "Introduction." In *School Desegregation* (1–18). Rotterdam, The Netherlands: SensePublishers.

Omi, M., and Winant, H. (2014). *Racial Formation in the United States.* New York, NY: Routledge.

Payne, R.K. (2005). *A Framework for Understanding Poverty.* 4th rev. ed. Highlands, Tex.: aha! Process.

Pearl, A. (1997). "Democratic Education as an Alternative to Deficit Thinking." In Valencia, R.R. (ed.). (2012). *The Evolution of Deficit Thinking: Educational Thought and Practice. Volume 19 of Stanford Series on Education and Public Policy.* Routledge.

Pei, A. (2018). *The Minority Experience. Navigating Emotional and Organizational Realities.* Downers Grove, IL: IVP Books, an imprint of InterVarsity Press.

Perkins, D.D., Crim, B., Silberman, P., and Brown, B. (2001). "Community Development as a Response to Community-Level Adversity: Ecological Theory and Research and Strengths-Based Policy." In LeChasseur, K. (2014). "Critical Race Theory and the Meaning of 'Community' in District Partnerships." *Equity and Excellence in Education* 47 (3). 305–320.

Porter, S.E. (2013). "Distinguishing a Christian Worldview and Supposed Cultural Absolutes." *McMaster Journal of Theology and Ministry* 15. 80.

"Privilege." In Dictionary.com. https://www.dictionary.com/browse/privilege?s=t.

Pulido, L. (2000). "Rethinking Environmental Racism: White Privilege and Urban Development in Southern California." *Annals of the Association of American Geographer* 90. 1, 12.

Rahn, W.M., Yoon, K.S., Garet, M., Lipson, S., and Loflin, K. (2003). "Geographies of Trust: Explaining Inter-Community Variation in General Social Trust Using Hierarchical Linear Modeling (HLM)." *Annual Conference of the American Association for Public Opinion Research* 16. Nashville, Tennessee.

"Religion and the Founding of the American Republic." (1998). Washington, DC: Library of Congress. https://lccn.loc.gov/2003557109.

Roediger, D.R. (2019). *How Race Survived US History: From Settlement and Slavery to the Obama Phenomenon*. New York: Verso.

Rogers, D., and Bowman, M. (2003). *Dismantling Racism: A Resource Book*. Western States Center.

Romme, A.G.L., and Van Witteloostuijn, A. (1999). "Circular Organizing and Triple Loop Learning. *Journal of Organizational Change Management* 12 (5). 439–454.

Rousmaniere, K. (2006). *Servants of the Poor: Teachers and Mobility in Ireland and Irish North America by Janet Nolan*. Wiley Online Library.

Rudolph, T.J., and Popp, E. (2010). "Race, Environment, and Interracial Trust." *The Journal of Politics* 72 (1). 74–89.

Russell, P.L. (1986). "Downtown's Downturn: A Historical Geography of the Phoenix, Arizona, Central Business District, 1890–1986." Master's thesis. Tempe, Arizona: Arizona State University.

Satterwhite, F.J.O., and Teng, S. (2007). *Culturally Based Capacity Building: An Approach to Working in Communities of Color for Social Change*. East Palo Alto, California: National Community Development Institute.

Schein, E. (1990). "Organizational Culture." *American Psychologist* 45 (2). 109–119.

Sensoy, Ö., and Ali-Khan, C. (2016). "Unpaving the Road to Hell: Disrupting Good Intentions and Bad Science about Islam and the Middle East." *Educational Studies* 52 (6). 506–520.

Sotero M. (2006). "A Conceptual Model of Historical Trauma: Implications for Public Health Practice and Research." *Journal of Health Disparities Research and Practice* 1 (1). 93–108.

Spencer-Oatey, H. (2008). *Culturally Speaking. Culture, Communication and Politeness Theory* (2nd ed.). London: Continuum.

Staats, C., Capatosto, K., Wright, R.A., and Contractor, D. (2015). *State of the Science: Implicit Bias Review 2015* (vol. 3). Columbus, Ohio: Kirwan Institute for the Study of Race and Ethnicity.

Straubhaar, R. (2015). "Will You Commit Class Suicide with Me?" https://www.opendemocracy.net/transformation/rolf-straubhaar/will-you-commit-class-suicide-with-me.

The Rise of Scientific Racial Ideology. Accessed July 24, 2020, https://msu.edu/~phill263/chart.html.

Tisby, J. (2019). *The Color of Compromise: The Truth About the American Church's Complicity in Racism*. Grand Rapids: Zondervan.

Valencia, R.R. (ed.). (2012). *The Evolution of Deficit Thinking: Educational Thought and Practice. Volume 19 of Stanford Series on Education and Public Policy*. Routledge.

Vander Zanden, J.W. (1959). "The Ideology of White Supremacy." *Journal of the History of Ideas*. 385–402.

Warren, M. (2005). "Communities and Schools: A New View of Urban Education Reform." *Harvard Educational Review* 75 (2). 133–173.

Warren, R. (2002). *The Purpose-Driven Life: What on Earth Am I Here For?* Grand Rapids, Michigan: Zondervan.

West, C. (2005). *Democracy Matters*. New York: Penguin Books.

Wexler, L.M., DiFluvio, G., and Burke, T.K. (2009). "Resilience and Marginalized Youth: Making a Case for Personal and Collective

Meaning-Making as Part of Resilience Research in Public Health." *Social Science and Medicine* 69 (4). 565–570.

Wiseman, T. (1996). "A Concept Analysis of Empathy." *Journal of Advanced Nursing* 23 (6). 1162–1167.

Yeo, F. (1997). "Teacher Preparation and Inner-City Schools: Sustaining Educational Failure." *The Urban Review* 29 (2). 127–143.

Yosso, T.J. (2005). "Whose Culture Has Capital? A Critical Race Theory Discussion of Community Cultural Wealth." *Race Ethnicity and Education* 8 (1). 69–91. doi: 10.1080/1361332052000341006.

www.ingramcontent.com/pod-product-compliance
Lightning Source LLC
Chambersburg PA
CBHW060358080526
44583CB00012B/373